SLAMMING THE DOOR

The Demolition of the Right to Asylum in the UK

AMNESTY INTERNATIONAL UNITED KINGDOM

Amnesty International United Kingdom
London

ISBN 1873328206

First Published April 1996

Amnesty International United Kingdom
99-119 Rosebery Avenue
London
EC1R 4RE

This book was researched and written by Richard Dunstan of the Refugee Office, Amnesty International United Kingdom.

Printed by Ennisfield Print and Design

Contents

Introduction

Forced out

Every year hundreds of thousands of desperate men, women and children flee their homeland to seek freedom from persecution.

Many have witnessed appalling human rights abuses as their governments crack down on dissent, and fear that they will be next on the list. Some have been individually targeted on account of their political activities, for exercising rights that many of us take for granted, or simply because they belong to an ethnic or religious minority. Others have sought safety abroad because their countries are racked by armed conflict or civil war.

Many have been forced to abandon not only their homes, their friends and their livelihood, but also their families: their lives are completely disrupted. And a lifetime's achievements, in education and employment, may be lost forever.

The political terror, oppression and conflict that lie behind these refugee movements are not confined to any one region or political system: in recent years people have fled human rights atrocities in Algeria, China, Colombia, Ethiopia, India, Iran, Kenya, Sri Lanka, Sudan, Turkey, and Zaire. New crises - Bosnia, Haiti, Nigeria and Rwanda - have created new movements, and old crises - Afghanistan, Iraq and Somalia - have deepened. Around the world, there are now some 15 million refugees.[1]

The vast majority of these refugees end up in neighbouring countries - often those least able to look after them. But a minority flee further afield, to Western Europe and to North America. Some do so in the hope of reaching a country with cultural, linguistic or historical links to their own, while others do so with the aim of joining relatives or friends already living there.

Unless and until oppressive governments stop persecuting and terrorising their citizens, such movements of people will continue: the refugee "problem" will not go away and cannot be ignored. But the international community's system of protecting such people depends on individual governments being willing to offer refuge to those who need it - in other words, on them keeping their doors open.

Closing the doors

Unfortunately, many governments have become less and less committed to the fundamental principles of refugee law which have been developed by the

---

[1] Source: Table 1 of Annex II, *The State of the World's Refugees 1995*, United Nations High Commissioner for Refugees.

international community since the Second World War, such as the 1951 UN Convention on Refugees. Some governments seem more concerned with limiting the number of asylum-seekers who reach their borders than providing proper asylum procedures, and least of all with stopping the human rights abuses which cause refugee movements. Increasingly, the importance of the right to seek asylum from persecution - enshrined in Article 14 of the Universal Declaration of Human Rights - is viewed as subsidiary to other political or economic concerns.

Moreover, it is often the countries with the greatest resources, to which comparatively few refugees flee, which have developed the most restrictive attitude towards asylum-seekers. This trend has been particularly pronounced among the relatively wealthy member states of the European Union who, since the mid-1980s, have worked together to develop restrictive asylum policies and practices. The aim of these common policies is clear: to reduce the number of refugees gaining entry, by preventing or deterring new arrivals of asylum-seekers, and by categorising certain types of asylum claim as "inadmissible" or otherwise not deserving full examination.

Closing Albion's door

Despite its oft-proclaimed commitment to the principles of international refugee law, and in particular to its obligations under the 1951 UN Convention, the British Government has embraced this restrictive approach to asylum policy. Since the mid-1980s, visa requirements have been imposed on nationals of all significant refugee-producing countries (eg Sri Lanka in 1985, Turkey in 1989, the former Yugoslavia in 1992 and Kenya in 1996), and have been enforced by the levying of fines on transport operators bringing passengers without a valid visa or passport.2 In order to avoid incurring fines, airlines and shipping companies now carry out checks on passengers' travel documents prior to embarkation, with a view to preventing those without the necessary visa from boarding. This works to prevent many would-be asylum-seekers - ineligible for visas - from travelling to the United Kingdom, other than by the use of forged documents and/or clandestine means of travel, both available (at a price) from unscrupulous profiteers.

In addition, the level of welfare benefits available to asylum-seekers while their application is under consideration has been reduced, and increasing numbers of asylum-seekers have been incarcerated in immigration detention centres and criminal prisons while their applications are examined, a measure which can

---

2 The Immigration (Carriers' Liability) Act 1987 provides for the imposition of a fine, currently £2,000 per passenger, on any transport operator bringing passengers lacking valid travel documents or a valid visa where one is required. Since the Act came into force, in March 1987, fines totalling over £89 million have been imposed on airlines and shipping companies.

only act as a deterrent to new arrivals. Those so detained may be held indefinitely, are not properly informed of the reasons for their detention, and have no effective opportunity to challenge those reasons before a court or similar body. Amnesty International has demonstrated that this lack of accountability, and the absence of proper judicial control over decisions to detain, results in arbitrary decision-making and unnecessary detentions. Since July 1993 the number of asylum-seekers so detained at any one time has more than doubled, and the average length of such detention has increased significantly.3

And in July 1993, following a seemingly orchestrated series of alarmist and misleading articles about "bogus refugees" in several pro-Government newspapers, the Government enacted new legislation - the Asylum & Immigration Appeals Act - which, whilst introducing new rights of appeal, provided for stricter application of the criteria for granting asylum and the rapid expulsion of rejected asylum-seekers. Even before the Act came into force, the Home Office Asylum Division's decision-making had become characterised by a "culture of disbelief" - a marked tendency to summarily dismiss asylum-seekers' claims as "unfounded" or "exaggerated". But since July 1993, despite no appreciable change in the nature or quality of asylum claims, the proportion of successful applications has fallen substantially (and to surprisingly uniform levels).

The 1993 Act also established special "fast track" procedures enabling the Home Office to seek to "pass the buck" by summarily returning asylum-seekers to "third" countries - that is, countries they transited through *en route* to the United Kingdom and where, it is held, they should seek asylum - without examining the merits of their fear of persecution and without any guarantee that the authorities of the "third" country in question are willing to do so. Amnesty International has repeatedly expressed its concern that this practice imposes immense hardship on those asylum-seekers unfortunate enough to fall within its scope and seriously compromises the Government's ability to fully uphold its obligations under international law.4

Slamming the door shut

By early 1995, however, it was apparent that the Government was considering yet further changes to its arrangements for dealing with asylum claims. In February 1995 the Home Office released details of a study of the existing asylum appeals mechanism, carried out in late 1994 by accountants KPMG Peat

---

3 On 31 January 1996, for example, a total of 733 asylum-seekers, including 49 women, were detained under Immigration Act powers; of these detainees, at least 255 were held in criminal prisons, and 110 had been held for longer than six months. For further information on Amnesty International's concerns on this issue, see *Prisoners Without a Voice: Asylum-seekers Detained in the United Kingdom* (2nd edition, May 1995).

4 For further information on Amnesty International's concerns on this issue, see *Playing Human Pinball: Home Office Practice in "Safe Third Country" Asylum Cases* (June 1995).

Marwick, including its recommendation for an erosion of the legal safeguards established in July 1993. In March 1995 the Home Secretary, Michael Howard MP, was widely reported to be considering proposals as diverse as the removal of oral appeal hearings in certain cases, the imposition of more visa regimes, the creation of a "white list" of countries presumed not to produce refugees, and a further "reduction" in the level of welfare benefits available to asylum-seekers. And the summer months saw a repetition of the build-up to the introduction of the 1993 Act, with pro-Government newspapers carrying a series of alarmist - and misleading - articles about "bogus asylum appeals".

Finally, after months of speculation, the Government formally announced two separate, but complementary, measures. Firstly, on 11 October 1995, during the Conservative Party Conference, the Secretary of State for Social Security, Peter Lilley MP, announced new Social Security Regulations, providing for the cessation of many asylum-seekers' entitlement to Income Support, Housing Benefit and other welfare benefits. The Regulations were published (in draft form) the following day, and were set to come into force on 8 January 1996, a timetable that did not allow for the Regulations to be debated and voted on by Parliament before their enactment. However, in late December 1995, following his receipt of a highly critical report on the Regulations by the government-appointed Social Security Advisory Committee (SSAC), which also recommended that the Regulations be abandoned, the Government announced that enactment would be delayed to allow for debates in Parliament. Following debates in the House of Commons (on 23 January) and House of Lords (on 30 January), and despite further trenchant criticism of the Regulations by the United Nations High Commissioner for Refugees (UNHCR), among others, the Regulations came into force on 5 February 1996.[5]

In flagrant disregard for the Government's obligations under international law, the Regulations deny access to the welfare benefits system by those individuals who, for legitimate and wholly understandable reasons, apply for asylum only after entering the United Kingdom, rather than immediately upon arrival. The Regulations also make inadequate provision for those individuals who become trapped in the United Kingdom due to a major change of circumstances (such as a coup or outbreak of civil war) in their own country. And, perhaps most damagingly of all, the Regulations deny access to the welfare benefits system by all those seeking to appeal against a refusal of their asylum claim.

In the meantime, in the Queen's Speech in mid-November 1995, the Government had also confirmed its intention to bring forward new legislation to "streamline" the handling of asylum applications. And on 30 November 1995, the Home Secretary, Michael Howard MP, published the Asylum & Immigra-

---

5 Full title: Social Security (Persons from Abroad) Miscellaneous Amendment Regulations 1996.

tion Bill, providing for significant changes to the asylum procedures established in July 1993.

Inter alia, the Bill - which at the time of writing remains under consideration by Parliament - provides for a substantial expansion of the scope of the truncated and accelerated appeal mechanism, established under the 1993 Act, for cases deemed to be "manifestly unfounded". In particular, it provides that this "fast track" appeal mechanism - which Amnesty International believes offers insufficient opportunity to challenge an unjust refusal - will be applied to cases of applicants from a list of supposedly "safe" countries deemed not to produce genuine refugees, and to those cases where - in the view of the Home Office - the circumstances which gave rise to the applicant's fear of persecution "no longer subsist". In Amnesty International's view, this can only increase the risk of unjust refusals going uncorrected and, ultimately, of genuine refugees being expelled to countries where they face persecution.

Furthermore, and perhaps most damagingly, the Bill provides for the abolition of the existing right to appeal *prior to expulsion* in those cases where the applicant arrives not directly from the country of persecution, but via one or more transit (or "third") countries. This raises the prospect of large numbers of asylum-seekers being summarily refused and expelled to countries through which they travelled *en route* to the United Kingdom, without *any* opportunity to challenge the refusal of their application and without any guarantee that the "third" country to which they are being expelled will accept responsibility for dealing with their asylum claim. This in turn raises the prospect of such individuals being successively expelled (or "chain removed") from one transit country to another, with the risk that some will be left "in orbit" between two or more countries unwilling to accept responsibility for them and that others will ultimately be returned to countries where the asylum procedures are seriously deficient or non-existent, and where they will face expulsion to the country of persecution. **6**

Amnesty International believes that the combination of these measures amounts to an effective demolition of the existing asylum process, and therefore to an abdication by the Government of its responsibilities under international law. As a signatory to the 1951 UN Convention on Refugees and other international instruments, the Government has a legal obligation to identify and protect all those asylum-seekers who have genuinely fled persecution, but this obligation can only be met fully if the procedures used to determine individual asylum claims are fair and satisfactory, *and if those fleeing persecution retain effective*

---

6 In addition, the Bill creates a new criminal offence of obtaining, or seeking to obtain, leave to enter or remain in the UK by deception; increases penalties for immigration offenders (both individuals and facilitators); and provides for criminal sanctions against companies employing illegal immigrants. However, in general, these provisions fall outside the scope of Amnesty International's work and are not dealt with in this report.

access to these procedures.

In Amnesty International's view, the Bill's implementation would result in a substantial diminution of the effectiveness of existing legal safeguards in the asylum process, thereby militating even further against the fair and satisfactory resolution of asylum claims. And the new Social Security Regulations, by denying many asylum applicants - including those unjustly refused asylum and seeking to overturn that refusal at appeal - the means to sustain themselves physically during the often lengthy periods of time that their application or appeal is under examination, may in any case render meaningless the existence of such legal safeguards.

This report sets out Amnesty International's principal concerns in respect of both the new Social Security Regulations which came into force on 5 February, and the Asylum & Immigration Bill, which seems likely to become law within the next few months. But it also contains Amnesty International's response to a number of arguments used recently by Government ministers and others to justify these two measures, as well as further information which the organisation believes is relevant to any serious discussion of the issues raised by the Government's obligations and intentions. In particular, it sets out Amnesty International's concern that the Asylum & Immigration Bill stems directly from a secretive - and therefore undemocratic - process aimed at the creation of a common, restrictive European Union asylum policy. It demonstrates that, in seeking to justify these measures, Government ministers have used "bogus" arguments and relied upon "bogus" statistics - to such an extent that Parliament and the public have been seriously misled. And it sets out the organisation's belief that, rather than eroding legal safeguards and denying access to the asylum process, the Government should be addressing the undeniably significant problems associated with having to deal with large numbers of asylum applications by taking steps to ensure faster and more efficient processing of asylum claims and appeals.

Legislative background: existing Home Office asylum procedures

On 26 July 1993 the Government enacted the Asylum & Immigration Appeals Act. Whilst providing for new rights of appeal, the Act was accompanied by new Immigration Rules on Asylum - since incorporated into the consolidated Immigration Rules (HC 395) - providing for stricter application of the criteria for granting asylum, and by Asylum Appeals (Procedure) Rules setting out strict time limits for the lodging, hearing and determination of appeals. In particular, the 1993 Act and Procedure Rules established a special "fast track" appeal mechanism - with extremely narrow time limits and limited-scope appeal hearings - for certain cases, namely: those where the applicant arrived at the United Kingdom's borders not directly from the country of persecution, but via one or more transit (or "third") countries; and those where, in the view of the Home Office, the asylum claim is "frivolous or vexatious".

All applications for asylum - whether made on arrival at a port or after entry to the United Kingdom - are considered and determined by officials in the Asylum Division of the Home Office's Immigration & Nationality Department. If, having considered the asylum claim and any representations or further information submitted on the applicant's behalf, the Asylum Division is satisfied that the applicant qualifies as a refugee under Article 1 of the 1951 UN Convention, then he or she will be granted asylum; otherwise, the application is refused. And, if the Asylum Division is not so satisfied, but accepts that there are "humanitarian or compassionate" reasons why the applicant should be allowed to remain in the United Kingdom, then he or she may be granted Exceptional Leave to Remain (ELR). However, under Paragraph 345 of the Immigration Rules, the application may be summarily refused, *without substantive consideration of the merits of the asylum claim*, if the applicant arrived not directly from the country of persecution but via one or more transit (or "third") countries and, in the view of the Home Office, he or she can be returned to one of those transit countries.[7]

Under the procedures established by the 1993 Act, all those refused asylum by the Asylum Division have a right of appeal to the independent Immigration Appellate Authority (IAA), part of the Lord Chancellor's Department.

According to the 1993 Act and Procedure Rules, appeals must normally be lodged within 10 working days of the refusal, and are heard by a single IAA Special Adjudicator, who must hear and determine the appeal within 42 days of it being lodged. In the event that the appeal is dismissed by the Special Adjudicator there is a further right of appeal, subject to leave and on a point of law only, to a three-member Immigration Appeals Tribunal (IAT). Similarly, in the event that the appeal is allowed by the Special Adjudicator, the Home Office can make a counter appeal against that decision to the IAT; in the event of no such counter appeal being made by the Home Office (or in the event that a counter appeal is made, but dismissed by the IAT), then the successful appellant will be recognised as a refugee and granted asylum.

However, in those cases where the application has been refused on "safe third country" grounds (ie, under Paragraph 345 of the Immigration Rules), or on the grounds that the asylum claim is "frivolous or vexatious", the appeal must be

---

[7] Amnesty International has repeatedly expressed its concern that application of Paragraph 345 of the Immigration Rules, and the associated "fast track" appeal mechanism, imposes immense hardship on those asylum-seekers unfortunate enough to fall within its scope and seriously compromises the upholding of the Government's obligations under international law. For further information, see *Playing Human Pinball: Home Office Practice in "Safe Third Country" Asylum Cases* (June 1995).

lodged within two working days of the refusal, the Special Adjudicator must hear and determine the appeal within seven working days of it being lodged, and there is no further right of appeal to the IAT.**8** In such cases, the *scope* of the appeal is also limited: in "safe third country" cases, for example, the only issue examined at the appeal is that of whether the "third country" in question is indeed "safe" for the individual in question, ie the appeal does not address the merits of the applicant's fear of persecution. Having heard the appellant's response to the refusal, the Special Adjudicator can either dismiss the appeal or, if he or she disagrees with the Home Office decision to refuse the asylum claim on "safe third country" grounds, refer the case back to the Home Office for substantive consideration of the merits of the applicant's fear of persecution. In the event that the appeal is dismissed by the Special Adjudicator, then the only further remedy available is the seeking of judicial review in the High Court.**9**

Once all appeal rights have been exhausted, all unsuccessful appellants are liable to removal (ie expulsion), either to their country of origin or, in "safe third country" cases, to one of the countries through which they passed in transit (normally the last transit country through which they passed before reaching the United Kingdom).

In May 1995 the Home Office introduced a pilot scheme (the "Short Procedure Pilot") aimed at reaching very quick decisions on "after entry" applications by nationals of Ghana, India, Nigeria, Pakistan, Poland, Romania and Uganda. (Sri Lanka was initially covered by the pilot scheme, but was subsequently dropped). Under this pilot scheme, applicants were given a short interview at the time of application, and any further information or representations had to be submitted within five days of the interview, after which a decision was made. The Home Office has confirmed that 100 per cent of the applicants dealt with under this pilot scheme were refused asylum.

In November 1995 the Home Office announced a two-fold extension of this "Short Procedure".**10** Since 27 November 1995, the scheme has covered "after entry" applicants from 35 countries, including Albania, Algeria, Bulgaria, Cameroon, Czech Republic, Egypt, Gambia, Ghana, Hungary, India, Ivory Coast, Nigeria, Pakistan, Poland, Romania, Senegal, Sierra Leone, the Slovak

---

8 The two-day limit on the lodging of an appeal in such cases applies only where the notice of refusal is served in person (in current practice, where the applicant is, at the time of refusal, detained under Immigration Act powers); otherwise, the 10-day limit applies.
9 However, unlike individual asylum appellants the Home Office does have a right to appeal to the IAT against a Special Adjudicator's decision not in its favour. Judicial review is a mechanism by which the High Court can test the validity of a decision by a lower court, or an administrative decision by a local authority or - as in asylum cases - a government department. However, it provides a procedural review only, ie it focuses not on the merits of the decision in question, but rather on whether the law and prescribed procedures have been followed.
10 By letter, dated 20 November 1995, from the Home Office Asylum Division to various refugee agencies.

Republic, Togo and Tunisia. And, since the end of November 1995, the scheme has also been applied to port applications made upon arrival at Gatwick airport. However, in this case the scheme is being applied to *all* nationalities except Afghanistan, Bosnia, Croatia (and the former Yugoslavia), the Gulf States (except Kuwait), Iran, Iraq, Liberia, Libya, Palestine, Rwanda and Somalia. It is surely no coincidence that these countries were the only applicant nationalities to be granted asylum or ELR in significant numbers in 1995.

The Home Office has stated that the aim of this short procedure is to produce initial decisions "within five weeks", compared to the current average of about nine months for a new claim.[11] While any reduction in overall decision times is to be welcomed, Amnesty International is concerned that, without the deployment of additional staff resources or other means of improving productivity, such a drastic reduction in decision times will only be achieved by a substantial reduction in the level of consideration given to the *individual* merits of each asylum claim dealt with under the Short Procedure, with an associated increase in the risk of unjust refusals.

---

11 Letter from the Home Office minister, Ann Widdecombe MP, in *The Independent,* 29 November 1995.

The new Social Security regulations

Background

Prior to 5 February 1996, all those seeking asylum in the United Kingdom were entitled to claim means-tested welfare benefits - including Income Support (although only at 90 per cent of the standard rate), Housing Benefit and Council Tax Benefit - while their asylum application was under consideration by the Home Office. This benefit entitlement was universal, in that it covered all asylum-seekers (and their dependants), regardless of whether their asylum application had been made on arrival at a port of entry, or after entering the United Kingdom (legally or otherwise) on another basis. And benefit entitlement continued during the period in which any appeal against a refusal of asylum was under consideration by the independent Immigration Appellate Authority.

The Social Security (Persons from Abroad) Miscellaneous Amendment Regulations 1996, which came into force on 5 February 1996, have ended the entitlement to Income Support, Housing Benefit and Council Tax Benefit of all those who apply for asylum after entering the United Kingdom. Under the Regulations, those persons who apply for asylum immediately upon arrival at a port retain entitlement to such benefits while awaiting an *initial* decision on their application by the Home Office. However, the Regulations also provide for the cessation of entitlement to such benefits for *all* asylum-seekers - ie, including those who apply for asylum upon arrival at a port - from the point at which they receive a negative decision from the Home Office. In other words, welfare benefits are no longer available to rejected asylum-seekers during any appeal (to the Immigration Appellate Authority) against the Home Office's refusal of their asylum claim.

The Regulations were first announced by the Secretary of State for Social Security, Peter Lilley MP, during his speech to the Conservative Party Conference on 11 October 1995, and were first published (in draft form) by the Department of Social Security (DSS) the following day. On the same day, the government-appointed Social Security Advisory Committee (SSAC), which examines all draft Social Security regulations and is empowered to make recommendations to the Secretary of State, invited comments on the draft Regulations by interested organisations and individuals.

At that time, the draft Regulations were set to come into force on 8 January 1996, a timetable that did not allow for the draft Regulations to be debated, and voted on, by Parliament. However, in late December, following his receipt of a highly critical report on the draft Regulations by the SSAC, Mr Lilley conceded a delay in enactment in order to allow for debates in Parliament.

In its submissions to the SSAC, Amnesty International argued that, in flagrant disregard for the Government's obligations under international law, the Regulations as drafted would unjustly deny access to the welfare benefits system by those individuals who, for legitimate and wholly understandable reasons, apply for asylum only *after* entering the United Kingdom, rather than immediately upon arrival; that the draft Regulations made inadequate provision for those individuals who become trapped in the United Kingdom due to a major change of circumstances (such as a coup) in their own country; and that the Regulations as drafted would unjustly deny access to the welfare benefits system by all those seeking to appeal against a refusal of their asylum claim, thereby seriously undermining the right of appeal established as recently as July 1993 under the Asylum & Immigration Appeals Act.

The SSAC report on the draft Regulations, published on 11 January 1996 (the same day that the Regulations were laid before Parliament), accepted that "by penalising all but a minority of asylum-seekers, *without regard to the strength or validity of their claim*", the draft Regulations were "arbitrary and unjust" and would have "drastic and unwelcome consequences" for "some of the most vulnerable and defenceless in our society". The SSAC report also noted that "apart from the extreme hardship that would be caused for so many, the proposed Regulations would also be operationally very cumbersome and raise many practical difficulties" and "would entail considerable administrative costs as well as substantial charges to local authority and other budgets outside Social Security". In particular, the SSAC noted the difficulties likely to be associated with serving notice of an interview or appeal hearing on asylum-seekers "without an address or funds". Concluding that "a more equitable and satisfactory approach ... would be to ensure faster and more efficient asylum procedures" the SSAC recommended that the draft Regulations be abandoned.1

However, the Government refused to accept the recommendation of the SSAC - or even to make amendments to the Regulations as originally drafted - and made only one concession to the SSAC's forthright criticisms: the abandonment of retrospective transitional arrangements that would have resulted in at least 13,000 asylum-seekers already in the system losing their existing benefit entitlement on the day the Regulations came into force. But for this concession, 13,000 vulnerable men, women and children would have been thrown into destitution on one single day. Following a short, late-night debate in the House of Commons, and despite further trenchant criticism of the Regulations by the United Nations High Commissioner for Refugees (UNHCR), among others, the Regulations came into force on 5 February 1996.

1 *Report by the Social Security Advisory Committee under Section 174(1) of the Social Security Administration Act 1992*, Cm 3062, January 1996. The SSAC received submissions from over 200 concerned organisations and individuals, including Amnesty International, the Refugee Council, the UN High Commissioner for Refugees, the Commission for Racial Equality, and the Refugee Legal Centre.

Amnesty International's concerns

It is Amnesty International's view that these Regulations will have an extremely serious and deleterious effect on the Government's fulfilment of its obligation under the 1951 UN Convention on Refugees and other international law, namely its obligation to identify and offer protection to all those seeking asylum in its territory who have genuinely fled persecution. For this obligation to be fully met, the procedures used to determine asylum claims must be fair and satisfactory, *and those fleeing persecution must have effective access to these procedures.* As the Office of the United Nations High Commissioner for Refugees (UNHCR) has stated: "it is trite to note that legal entitlements may be rendered ineffective if individual asylum-seekers are unable to sustain themselves physically during the sometimes lengthy period in which their status is determined ... Within the humanitarian spirit of the [1951 UN] Convention lies a State's obligation to ensure that asylum-seekers enjoy basic subsistence support to sustain them in dignity during this waiting period".**2**

And, as the Home Office's own research has concluded, the overwhelming majority of genuine refugees are not financially independent when they arrive in the United Kingdom, and have "immediate needs for food, clothing and housing".**3** Accordingly, a denial of such individuals' means of meeting their obvious needs for food, shelter and other essentials can only act as a serious impediment to their access to the asylum-determination procedures. And the Government cannot fully meet its international obligations while taking steps that have the effect, if not the intention, of restricting the opportunities for individuals fleeing persecution to seek and obtain protection in the United Kingdom.

The Regulations: ending the benefit of "after entry" asylum-seekers

The Regulations provide for the curtailment of entitlement to income support and other benefits for those who apply for asylum after entering the United Kingdom. This includes persons with leave to enter or remain in the United Kingdom (eg as a visitor or student) at the time of application, having entered in possession of a valid visa, as well as persons who have overstayed such leave and persons who entered the country clandestinely and therefore unlawfully (ie, "illegal entrants").

As the Department of Social Security's own Explanatory Memorandum on the Regulations itself makes clear, such persons may claim asylum "because of a genuine change of circumstances either in their country of origin (wars, coups, etc), *or* in their own circumstances (ie fresh information that they would

---

2 Representations to the SSAC by the London office of UNHCR, November 1995.
3 *The Settlement of Refugees in Britain,* Home Office Research Study 141, 1995.

personally be at risk if they returned)." However, while the Regulations provide for an exemption to the curtailment of benefit entitlement in those cases where the asylum application is made "within three months" of a declaration by the Secretary of State that their home country has undergone "such a fundamental change in circumstances that he would not normally order the return of a person to that country" (eg a coup), they do *not* provide for such an exemption to the curtailment of benefit entitlement in those cases where the asylum application is prompted by a change in the applicant's *individual* circumstances (ie fresh information that he or she would personally be at risk). In Amnesty International's view, such inconsistency is grossly unfair and cannot be justified.

Furthermore, the limitation of the scope of the "fundamental change" exemption to those who apply for asylum *within three months* of the Secretary of State's declaration is, in Amnesty International's view, an arbitrary one that will inevitably result in the unjust denial of benefits to needy individuals with genuine asylum claims. The circumstances giving rise to a well-founded fear of persecution that stem from a particular "fundamental change" such as a military coup often persist for many months or even years after the date of that event, and nationals of the country in question in the United Kingdom at the time of the "fundamental change", and therefore at the time of the Secretary of State's declaration (which would presumably follow shortly afterwards), may have no particular need to apply for asylum at that point (because they already have leave to enter or remain for some considerable time ahead). As the following example illustrates, such individuals (who cannot be assumed familiar with the relevant benefit regulations) may wait until that leave is about to expire before submitting, in desperation, an application for asylum.

Mr A, a Sudanese national, came to the United Kingdom in April 1986 to undertake post-graduate study, supported financially by the Sudanese government, and was accordingly granted leave to remain until 10 April 1990. Following the overthrow of the Sudanese government by a military coup in June 1989, Mr A feared returning to Sudan but hoped that the situation would improve before the expiry of his leave to remain. In late-1989, however, the new Sudanese authorities terminated Mr A's student grant and from that time on he survived off his meagre savings and the occasional charity of British academic colleagues; at the same time Mr A learned that a number of his former academic colleagues in Sudan had been detained and tortured by the new military authorities. By the beginning of April 1990 the situation in Sudan had worsened and, after seeking the advice of Amnesty International on 8 April, Mr A applied for asylum in person at the Home Office Asylum Division in Croydon on 9 April 1990, the day before his leave to remain expired. On 14 December 1992 - more than 34 months later - Mr A was granted asylum; he remained dependent upon Income Support and other benefits until obtaining employment in

November 1990, a period of seven months.

Moreover, and perhaps most damagingly, the DSS Explanatory Memorandum on the Regulations omits to mention, and the Regulations make no allowance for, the fact that those genuinely fleeing persecution may have legitimate and wholly understandable reasons - *other than a change of circumstances* - for applying for asylum only after entering the country, rather than immediately upon arrival.

Such individuals are not, of course, familiar with the complexities of the United Kingdom's immigration law or benefits regulations. And, having experienced state oppression first hand - and possibly still traumatised as a result - they may be fearful of authority and hopeful of seeking the help and support of friends, relatives and advice agencies before putting their fate in the hands of officialdom. As the following examples illustrate, many enter the country lawfully, using valid travel documents, while others enter clandestinely or using forged travel documents: the imposition of visa regimes on refugee-producing countries (see introduction), and their enforcement by the levying of fines on transport companies who bring passengers lacking the necessary visa, has forced more and more refugees to resort to the use of forged documents and/or clandestine means of travel in order to make their escape to the United Kingdom. In this respect, it should be noted that such individuals are often advised by the agent providing the forged documents or means of travel to enter the country before seeking asylum.

Mr B fled from Sri Lanka to the United Kingdom, accompanied by his wife and young daughter, in January 1990. As a prominent lawyer and human rights activist, Mr B had become a principal target for "death squads" linked to the security forces and responsible for a wave of killings of lawyers engaged in human rights work; in the weeks leading up to his flight from Sri Lanka a number of Mr B's clients had been shot dead, and his legal clerk had been abducted and raped. Following representations by Amnesty International and the Sri Lankan Bar Association, Mr B was issued with a visit visa by the British High Commission, and on 16 January 1990 he used this visa to enter the United Kingdom at Heathrow airport. Mr B then sought the advice of Amnesty International, and on 19 January 1990 Amnesty International's Refugee Office submitted an asylum claim on his behalf to the Home Office Asylum Division. On 11 March 1992 - almost 26 months later - Mr B was granted asylum; throughout this period, he and his family remained dependent upon Income Support and other benefits.

Mr C fled from Iran to the United Kingdom in November 1991. A lecturer in engineering at Tehran University, Mr C had been arrested in 1983 and sentenced to 15 years' imprisonment for his non-violent opposition to the Islamic government. During the first five months of his imprisonment, Mr C was subjected to such severe torture that he suffered a near-fatal heart attack, a broken collarbone (from prolonged suspension by the arms), a ruptured eardrum (from beatings to the ears), and almost total loss of vision in his right eye (from beatings to the head). On 1 November 1991 - shortly before a visit to Tehran of the UN Special Representative on Iran - Mr C was released from Evin prison on 15 days' prison leave, his family having pledged to return him to prison at the end of this period.4

Mr C's family then smuggled him (in the boot of a car) across the border to Turkey, where they purchased a forged Spanish passport from an agent. Mr C then used this document to enter the United Kingdom, at Heathrow airport, on 29 November 1991; the agent travelled with him and took possession of the forged document immediately after entry was completed (presumably for re-use). Mr C then sought the advice of Amnesty International, and on 5 December 1991 he applied for asylum in person at the Home Office Asylum Division in Croydon. On 18 March 1992 - determination of his claim having been expedited, at Amnesty International's prompting, in order that Mr C's wife could flee Iran before herself being detained in lieu of her husband - Mr C was granted asylum; throughout this period, he remained dependent upon Income Support and other benefits.

Under the new Regulations, applicants such as Mr B and Mr C are no longer entitled to claim Income Support and other benefits, as the Regulations make no allowance for such circumstances. In Amnesty International's view, this creates an unjustifiable and, in most cases, insurmountable barrier between such individuals and the United Kingdom's asylum-determination procedures. Clearly, without an entitlement to benefits, such individuals - unless they are of independent means - will not be able to sustain themselves physically during the average period of almost nine months that it currently takes for the Home Office to reach an initial decision.5 Accordingly, the enactment of the Regulations has resulted in a serious diminution of the Government's ability to fully meet its obligations under the 1951 Convention on Refugees and other international law.

Moreover, it is clear that a very large proportion - if not the vast majority - of *genuine* "after entry" asylum-seekers make their application within a few days or weeks of entering the United Kingdom, for reasons such as those illustrated by the cases of Mr B and Mr C, rather than after a period of months or even years.6

---

4 It is the common practice of the Iranian authorities to so release large numbers of political prisoners on temporary leave during visits to Iran by UN human rights officials.
5 In the latter half of 1995 (the most recent period for which figures are available), the average time taken by the Home Office to reach an initial decision on a new asylum claim was 8.9 months. Source: *Hansard* (House of Commons), 8 February 1996, col. 310 (written answer).

And, as illustrated by the case of Mr A, others apply for asylum after some time in the United Kingdom due to a change of circumstances in their own country. Amnesty International can see no reason why such persons should be treated differently, in respect of benefit entitlement, to those who apply for asylum immediately upon arrival at a port of entry. In short, an asylum applicant's manner of entry - or attempted entry - to the United Kingdom has no bearing on the merits or legitimacy of his or her asylum claim.

In seeking to justify the new Regulations' distinction between "port" applicants and "after entry" applicants, Mr Lilley has relied heavily upon his claim that "after entry" asylum applications are inherently of less merit than "port" asylum applications, and that therefore "after entry" applicants are less deserving of welfare benefits. In his formal response to the SSAC's report on the Regulations, Mr Lilley stated that the proportion of those granted asylum is "lower for in-country [ie, after entry] applicants", a claim he subsequently repeated in the Commons debate on the Regulations.

Of course, even if this were true, Mr Lilley's argument does not address the question of what will happen to those genuine and needy "after entry" applicants who *are* deserving of both asylum and welfare benefits. In the four-year period 1992-95, a total of 3,445 "after entry" applicants were granted asylum, compared with a total of 1,385 "port" applicants. In other words, of the total of 4,830 individuals granted asylum in the past four years, the vast majority (71.3 per cent) were "after entry" applicants. It seems reasonable to conclude that each and every one of these 3,445 genuine refugees had good reasons for applying for asylum after entering the United Kingdom, rather than immediately upon arrival, but, if the Regulations had been in force during this period, none of them would have qualified for Income Support and other benefits while their asylum claim was under consideration by the Home Office. And, as the Home Office's own research has demonstrated, the overwhelming majority of these 3,445 genuine refugees were not financially independent, and were therefore reliant upon Income Support, Housing Benefit and other welfare benefits to meet their needs for food and shelter during that waiting period.

In fact, the Home Office's own figures show that Mr Lilley's argument is groundless. In each of the past four years the recognition rate (ie the proportion of cases fully examined and decided in which asylum was granted) among "after entry" applicants was actually *higher* than that among "port" applicants. In 1992,

---

6 According to Home Office figures, 37% of all "after entry" applicants make their asylum application within four weeks of entering the UK, 47% apply within two months of entering the UK, and 74% apply within six months. It should be noted, however, that even these figures are distorted by the inclusion of both those individuals applying for asylum some considerable time after first entering the UK (due to a change of circumstances in their own country), and those individuals making an unfounded asylum application (as a means of avoiding deportation on other grounds) many months or even years after entering the UK. Source: *Hansard* (House of Commons), 30 November 1995, col. 885 (written answer).

the recognition rate among "after entry" applicants was 6.6 per cent, while that among "port" applicants was 4.9 per cent; in 1993, the recognition rate among "after entry" applicants was 12.8 per cent, while that among "port" applicants was 4.3 per cent; and in 1994, the recognition rate among "after entry" applicants was 4.9 per cent, while that among "port" applicants was 4.7 per cent. Overall, during the three-year period 1992-94 the total proportion of "after entry" applicants granted asylum after full consideration of their asylum claim (7.96 per cent) was almost twice that of "port" applicants (4.65 per cent).**7**

Similarly, in 1995, not only did the vast majority (73.3 per cent) of the 1,295 individuals granted asylum by the Home Office apply "after entry", but the recognition rate among "after entry" applicants was 6.57 per cent, while that among "port" applicants was 3.85 per cent.**8**

In seeking to justify the Regulations, Mr Lilley has also argued that all those who apply for asylum after entering the United Kingdom will previously have had to demonstrate (to an Immigration Officer) that they can support themselves financially during their stay in the United Kingdom. In rejecting the SSAC's criticisms and recommendations, Mr Lilley claimed that "on arrival in this country all those from the main [refugee-producing] countries will have been interviewed by the immigration authorities, questioned about their intentions in visiting the United Kingdom and asked to confirm that they have the means to support themselves without recourse to public funds".**9** However, this argument ignores the many valid reasons why many genuine refugees make their asylum application only after entering the United Kingdom, rather than immediately upon arrival. As the SSAC concluded: "lack of knowledge of the procedures, arriving in a confused and frightened state, language difficulties or fear of officialdom may all be insuperable barriers to making any kind of approach to the authorities at [the] port of entry".

As already noted above, in the four-year period 1992-95 the Home Office granted asylum to a total of 3,445 "after entry" applicants, and it seems reasonable to conclude that each and every one of these genuine refugees had valid reasons for applying for asylum only after entering the United Kingdom. Of course, in some of these cases the individual will already have been in the United Kingdom - quite legitimately - on another basis, and will have applied for

---

7 Source for all 1992-94 figures: Home Office Statistical Bulletin 15/95, Tables 4.1, 4.2 & 4.3.
8 Source for 1995 figures: *Hansard* (House of Commons), 8 February 1996, col. 309 (written answer). The recognition rates amongst cases that have been subjected to full consideration, as cited here, are the most relevant comparative figures in this context, but even if those cases that have been refused without full consideration of the asylum claim - namely those refused on "safe third country" grounds (under Paragraph 345 of the Immigration Rules) and those refused for failure to provide evidence to support the asylum claim within a reasonable period (under Paragraph 340 of the Immigration Rules) - are included in this analysis the recognition rate amongst "after entry" cases in 1995 was 5.67 per cent, while the recognition rate among "port" cases was 3.36 per cent.
9 Paragraph 17 of the Government's formal response to the SSAC report on the Regulations, Cm 3062.

asylum due to a significant change of circumstances in his or her country. And, as illustrated by the case of Mr A, many of these individuals will have fallen outside the scope of the Regulations' "fundamental change" safeguard.

In other cases - as illustrated by the example of Mr B - the individual will have been examined on entry by an Immigration Officer but, for some or all of the valid reasons described above, will have given evasive or misleading answers to any questions posed by the Immigration Officer, and these will have been accepted by the Immigration Officer. And in many other cases - as illustrated by the example of Mr C - the individual will have used a manner of entry that by-passed any examination by an Immigration Officer.

As described above, Mr C entered the United Kingdom at Heathrow airport using a false Spanish passport, and applied for asylum a few days later after seeking the advice and assistance of Amnesty International. Only 28 days previously, Mr C had been incarcerated in Iran's most notorious prison, where he had been subjected to repeated and brutal torture. In the intervening period, he had been briefly united with the wife and family he had not seen for eight years, smuggled over the Iranian border in the boot of a car, and then flown to London accompanied by - and under the instructions of - an unfamiliar agent. And, of course, as an apparent national of an European Union member state, Mr C was not subjected to any examination or questioning as he passed through immigration control at Heathrow.

At the time of his arrival in the United Kingdom - and indeed for many months afterwards - Mr C was in an extremely traumatised state: still suffering horribly from his physical injuries sustained at the hands of Iranian torturers, Mr C also bore tremendous psychological scars from his eight years in prison, where he had seen many fellow inmates summarily executed. It is perhaps not surprising, therefore, that Mr C acted as he did. In doing so, of course, Mr C was simply following the instructions given to him both by his family in Iran, and by the agent who not only arranged his passage to the United Kingdom, but travelled with him in order to reclaim Mr C's forged Spanish passport for re-use.

And yet, according to Mr Lilley's argument, Mr C did not deserve to receive welfare benefits while he awaited the Home Office's determination of his asylum claim, a process which, but for the unusual intervention of Amnesty International (in order to enable Mr C's wife and family to flee Iran), could well have taken 18 months or even longer.10 Indeed, if Mr C were to arrive in the United Kingdom tomorrow, and apply for asylum just as he did in 1991, he would not be entitled to welfare benefits during the nine months that, on average, the Home Office is currently taking to determine an asylum

---

10 At the time of Mr C's arrival in the UK, the Home Office was taking an average of 17.5 months to determine an asylum application, and delays of two years or more were not uncommon.

application. Accordingly, with the enactment of the new Social Security Regulations it is difficult to envisage how any person such as Mr C will in future be able to seek, and obtain, asylum in the United Kingdom.

The Regulations: ending benefit entitlement from the point of refusal of asylum

The Regulations provide for the cessation of entitlement to Income Support and other benefits for *all* asylum applicants at the point where they receive a negative decision from the Home Office. This includes all those persons who apply for asylum immediately upon arrival at a port of entry who, unlike "after entry" applicants, retain entitlement to benefits from the time of application, as well as any individuals covered by the "fundamental change" exemption.

The determination of asylum applications is a difficult process, relying heavily on an evaluation of statements (by the applicant) that are not always susceptible to proof, and on an objective assessment of the political and human rights situation in countries that are often undergoing rapid and complex change. It is therefore inevitable that, in determining thousands of asylum applications each year, the Home Office Asylum Division will make errors of fact or judgement, and that these errors will lead to a not inconsiderable number of unjust refusals. An effective appeals mechanism is essential to the rectification of such unjust refusals and, accordingly, to the upholding of the Government's obligations under international law. And, as UNHCR has emphasised, an *effective* right of appeal includes "humanitarian welfare to support access to that right".

In rejecting the criticisms and recommendations of the Social Security Advisory Committee, Mr Lilley made much play of the fact that, according to official figures for 1994, "the decision to refuse [asylum] is overturned in only 4 per cent of appeal cases". However, it is important to recognise that in 1994 this "4 per cent" amounted to 95 men and women (plus their dependants).[11] In other words, but for the existence of the appeal mechanism created in 1993 (under the Asylum & Immigrations Appeal Act), the Government would have breached the 1951 UN Convention on Refugees on at least 95 occasions in 1994 alone.

For example, Mr D fled from Congo to the United Kingdom in January 1994, and applied for asylum immediately upon arrival at Dover seaport. The Home Office refused his application on 25 February 1994, but Mr D appealed against this decision to the Immigration Appellate Authority (IAA) and on 15 July 1994 the appeal was allowed by an IAA Special Adjudicator. On 1 August 1994 - over five months after the initial, wrongful refusal of his application - Mr D was granted asylum by the Home Office; throughout this period, Mr D remained dependent upon Income Support and other benefits.

---

11 Source: Home Office Statistical Bulletin 15/95, Table 8.3.

There can be no question that this cessation of benefit entitlement from the point of refusal creates a wholly unjustifiable and, in most cases, insurmountable barrier between those wrongly refused asylum and the existing asylum appeals mechanism. According to the Home Office's own figures, the average period between the refusal of an asylum application and the determination of the applicant's appeal to the IAA is currently just under 10 months.[12] Clearly, those without independent means have no chance of sustaining themselves physically for such a lengthy period of time, and the impact of the Regulations will inevitably lead to such individuals failing to pursue appeals to the IAA. In other words, the enactment of the Regulations is certain to result in unjust refusals going uncorrected and, ultimately, in breaches of the 1951 UN Convention on Refugees. In Amnesty International's view, this is unacceptable, whatever the numbers involved. As the former Cabinet minister, Peter Brooke MP, said during the House of Commons debate on the Regulations: "are the four per cent to be penalised because others, with whom they have no connection save that of category, are expected to fail?"[13]

The lack of alternative arrangements

The Government's failure to make alternative provision for the welfare of those asylum-seekers not entitled to benefits under the Regulations, which can only result in significant numbers of needy men, women and children being left in destitution, contrasts markedly with the arrangements in comparable European countries. In Denmark, Germany and the Netherlands, all asylum-seekers are housed in reception centres or refugee hostels where their basic needs (such as meals and clothing) are provided for, sometimes in kind, throughout the period that their asylum application is under consideration (including any appeal).

In Denmark, for example, asylum-seekers are accommodated in about 80 reception centres, located throughout the country and run by the Danish Red Cross on behalf of the Immigration Department. Each centre accommodates between 50 and 200 asylum-seekers. Meals and other basic needs are provided in the accommodation centres and, if the asylum-seeker does not have independent means, a clothing allowance and "pocket money" is paid to him or her by the Immigration Department.

In Germany, each *Land* is legally obliged to receive a certain proportion of newly-arrived asylum-seekers and to maintain reception centres providing sufficient places to accommodate its quota. There are about 50 reception centres located throughout the country, each accommodating between 500 and 1,800 asylum-seekers, and the day-to-day running of the centres is generally contracted out to private companies or the German Red Cross. In some centres, asylum-seekers are provided with ready-made meals, while in others they have access to kitchens where they can prepare their own meals. All other essential

---

12 In the latter half of 1995 (the most recent period for which figures are available), the average time taken by the Home Office and the Immigration Appellate Authority to hear and determine an asylum appeal was 9.8 months. Source: *Hansard* (House of Commons), 8 February 1996, col. 310 (written answer).

13 *Hansard* (House of Commons), 23 January 1996, col. 251.

personal items - such as clothing - are generally provided in kind, although a small allowance is also paid to many asylum-seekers. After 12 months, however, asylum-seekers are entitled to the standard level of welfare benefits available to all needy residents.

In the Netherlands, all asylum-seekers admitted to the full asylum procedure (after an initial screening at the port) are accommodated in one of about 25 reception centres, located throughout the country and holding up to 800 asylum-seekers. Meals are provided in the centres, but in addition asylum-seekers receive a small allowance for personal items.

Postscript

Between 5 February and early March 1996, at least 300 asylum-seekers are reported to have been denied Social Security benefits under these new Regulations, with many being forced to sleep in churches or emergency night shelters. For example, Ms E, a Zairean national, applied for asylum in person at the Home Office on 8 February, a matter of hours after entering the United Kingdom at Waterloo railway station using a forged Greek passport (ie. in a very similar manner to Mr C, above); as an "after entry" asylum applicant, Ms E has been denied Income Support and other benefits.[14] As this report went to print, the Regulations were the subject of an application for judicial review in the High Court, brought by the Joint Council for the Welfare of Immigrants. However, two local authorities, Wesminster City Council and Hammersmith and Fulham Borough Council, have abandoned similar legal challenges after the Government confirmed that it would provide 80 per cent relief for the additional costs that these and other local authorities will incur as the result of the new Regulations.[15]

---

14 "Asylum rules to deter refugees", *The Guardian*, 7 March 1996.
15 "Ministers retreat on the costs of asylum", *The Independent*, 6 March 1996.

The Asylum & Immigration Bill

Introduction

The Asylum & Immigration Bill, published on 30 November 1995, provides for significant changes to the Government's arrangements for dealing with applications for asylum in the United Kingdom. *Inter alia*, the Bill provides (in Clause 1) for a substantial extension of the scope of the truncated and accelerated appeal mechanism - established under the Asylum & Immigration Appeals Act 1993 - for cases deemed to be "manifestly unfounded". In particular, it provides that this "fast track" appeal mechanism will be applied to cases of rejected applicants from a "white list" of supposedly "safe" countries deemed not to produce genuine refugees, and to those cases where - in the view of the Home Office - the circumstances which gave rise to the applicant's fear of persecution "no longer subsist". Furthermore, new rules of procedure for such "fast track" appeals - not yet published - may well abolish the right to an *oral* appeal hearing in some or all of these cases (ie such appeals will be determined on the papers only).

Perhaps of most concern to Amnesty International, however, the Bill also provides (in Clauses 2 and 3) for the abolition of the existing right to appeal *prior to expulsion* in those cases where the applicant arrives not directly from the country of persecution, but via one or more transit (or "third") countries (hereafter referred to as "safe third country" cases).

In addition, the Bill creates an additional criminal offence of obtaining, or seeking to obtain, leave to enter or remain in the United Kingdom by deception; increases penalties for immigration offenders (both individuals and facilitators); and provides for criminal sanctions against companies employing illegal immigrants. However, in general these provisions fall outside the scope of Amnesty International's work and are not addressed in this report.

The origins of the Bill

The first thing that must be said about the Bill is that it forms part of a secretive - and therefore undemocratic - process aimed at the harmonisation of asylum policy within the European Union - ie, the creation of a common European Union asylum policy. For, contrary to the pledge of the Home Secretary, Michael Howard MP, to last October's Conservative Party Conference that "immigration policy will be decided here in Britain, and not in Brussels", the two main elements of the Bill - the creation of the so-called "white list" and the effective abolition of the right to appeal in "safe third country" cases - are drawn directly from European Union (EU) agreements, drafted by an obscure group of EU home affairs officials and signed by the Home Secretary or his predecessor at meetings of the EU Council of Ministers.

The creation of the so-called "white list", for example, is specifically provided for in the EU *Resolution on Manifestly Unfounded Applications for Asylum* and the EU *Conclusions on Countries in which there is Generally No Serious Risk of Persecution*, both signed by the then Home Secretary, Kenneth Clarke MP, and his EU counterparts at the December 1992 meeting of the EU Justice & Home Affairs Council in London.

Similarly, the effective abolition of appeal rights in "safe third country" cases is a key provision of the EU *Resolution on Minimum Guarantees for Asylum Procedures*, signed by Mr Howard and his EU counterparts at the June 1995 meeting of the EU Justice & Home Affairs Council in Luxembourg. This Resolution also provides (in Paragraph 31) that "Member States will take account of [the principles set out in this Resolution] in the case of all proposals for changes to their national legislation [and] will strive to bring their national legislation into line with these principles by 1 January 1996". A number of EU member states (eg Denmark, Finland, France, Germany and the Netherlands) have already done so, while others (eg Portugal and now the United Kingdom) are in the process of doing so.

These EU Resolutions and Conclusions were drawn up in secret by a group of EU home affairs officials, known as the Ad Hoc Group Immigration from the time of its formation in October 1986 until the coming into force of the Maastricht Treaty in 1993, since when it has been known as Steering Group 1 (Asylum and Immigration). This is one of three Steering Groups - the others being SG 2 (Police & Customs) and SG 3 (Judicial Control) - reporting to the K4 Committee of senior officials, which performs a coordinating role with regard to activities in the area of Justice and Home Affairs, the so-called "Third Pillar" of intergovernmental cooperation under the Maastricht Treaty.[1]

None of these documents has been debated - let alone approved -by the British Parliament. Indeed, it appears that until recently most MPs - including front-bench opposition MPs - were unaware of the documents' existence. In fact, the process is so secretive that in July 1992 the then Home Secretary, Kenneth Clarke MP, had to be informed of it by a *Guardian* journalist some four months after taking office. And yet there can be no question that the process that has produced these documents is intended to produce a common EU asylum policy. As Kenneth Clarke candidly conceded to the *Guardian* in 1992: "I'm amazed that British ministers have been allowed to get away with it for so long".[2]

While Amnesty International does not object in principle to the aim of

---

1 Since the signing in 1986 of the Single European Act, the EU member states have been working together on measures for the establishment of a single market for goods, persons and capital, and the associated abolition of checks at internal borders. Among these measures have been those relating to the control of immigration from outside the EU, including the handling of asylum applications, and the EU Resolutions and Conclusions described here are the product of this process.
2 "Secrecy over immigration stuns Clarke", *The Guardian*, 2 July 1992.

harmonising asylum policies and practices within the EU, the organisation is concerned that, to date, the process has resulted in the adoption of unsatisfactory common standards that fall short of international norms. Most EU governments seem increasingly preoccupied with reducing the number of refugees and asylum-seekers allowed to enter their territory, rather than with ensuring respect for the fundamental principles of refugee protection, and this has resulted in the creation of various complex and time-consuming "screening out" procedures and the setting up of separate, accelerated appeal mechanisms for specific categories of asylum claims - such as "manifestly unfounded" or "safe third country" cases - deemed not to merit full examination.

In most cases these new procedures lack certain essential safeguards and, accordingly, they provide greatly reduced levels of protection to genuine refugees. Individual EU governments have then pressed for these standards to be reflected, as part of the harmonisation process, in the EU Resolutions and Conclusions drawn up by the K4 Committee. And, as described above, these EU Resolutions and Conclusions, although technically not legally binding, have then shaped new national legislation (or changes to existing legislation and practice) in other EU member states. In short, the harmonisation process has resulted in an erosion of the standard of protection to the *lowest common level*.

And, of course, if relatively wealthy and powerful governments (which receive only a relatively small proportion of the total number of refugees in the world) take it upon themselves to erode the standards of refugee protection, there is a real risk that other countries will feel inclined to follow that example. Indeed, a number of non-EU countries (eg Switzerland) have already introduced new asylum legislation based on the K4 Committee's Resolutions and Conclusions.

Since the late 1980s, Amnesty International has repeatedly called on the governments of all EU member states to ensure that the harmonisation of asylum policy and practice within the EU does not result in a lowering of the level of protection to asylum-seekers, and has set out its recommendations for a common set of legal and procedural safeguards - drawn from international standards - that should be included in any asylum-determination process. The organisation very much regrets that its appeals have gone almost entirely unheeded.[3]

---

[3] For further information, see these Amnesty International reports: *Europe: the need for minimum standards in asylum procedures* (June 1994); *Europe: harmonisation of asylum policy* (November 1992); *Europe: human rights and the need for a fair asylum policy* (November 1991); and *Harmonisation of asylum policy in Europe: Amnesty International's concerns* (April 1990).

Clause 1 of the Bill - the provisions

Schedule 2 of the Asylum & Immigration Appeals Act 1993 created a truncated and accelerated appeals mechanism for those cases where the asylum claim has been refused on the grounds that it is "without foundation", ie where the asylum claim has been refused on "safe third country" grounds, or where - in the Home Office's view - the claim is "frivolous or vexatious". In line with the EU Resolutions and Conclusions described above, Clause 1(2) of the Bill amends Schedule 2 of the 1993 Act so as to extend the scope of this "fast track" appeals mechanism to *seven* categories of cases:

i)   those where the applicant is from a "white list" of designated countries where - in the view of the Home Secretary - "there is in general no serious risk of persecution";

ii)   those where, on arrival in the United Kingdom, the applicant "failed to produce a passport without giving a reasonable explanation for his failure to do so", or "produced a passport which was not in fact valid and failed to inform the [immigration] officer of that fact";

iii) those where, in the view of the Home Office, the applicant has not shown a fear of persecution "by reason of [his or her] race, religion, nationality, membership of a particular social group, or political opinion" (the wording of Article 1 of the 1951 UN Convention);

iv)   those where the applicant *has* shown such a fear but, in the view of the Home Office, "the fear is manifestly unfounded or the circumstances which gave rise to the fear no longer subsist";

v)   those where the asylum application is made at any time after the applicant has been refused leave to enter the United Kingdom, where the applicant has been recommended for deportation by a court, or where the applicant is an "illegal entrant" (ie where he or she has entered the United Kingdom without permission);

vi)   those where, in the view of the Home Office, the asylum claim is "manifestly fraudulent, or any of the evidence adduced in its support is manifestly false"; and

vii) those where, in the view of the Home Office, the asylum claim is "frivolous or vexatious".

Clause 1 of the Bill: Amnesty International's concerns

At the time of writing, it is difficult to predict the *precise* implications of Clause 1 of the Bill, as the Government has yet to indicate in detail how this expanded "fast track" mechanism will operate in practice. It is not clear, for example, whether these "fast track" appeals will be subject to the same narrow time limits of the existing "fast track" mechanism, or whether new time limits will apply. Home Office ministers have indicated that the Government will in due course bring forward new Procedure Rules for all "fast track" appeals, and until these are published all comments on the likely impact of Clause 1 must be provisional.4

However, even without sight of the associated Procedure Rules, it is clear that the implementation of Clause 1 is likely to result in very large numbers of asylum applicants having an inadequate opportunity to challenge an unjust refusal. Not only are such "fast track" appeals likely to be subject to unacceptably narrow time limits, but the opportunities to contest the Home Office's reasons for refusal at an oral hearing before an IAA Special Adjudicator - and, in the event of the appeal being dismissed, to make a further appeal on a point of law to the Immigration Appeal Tribunal - are likely to be restricted.

Under the existing Procedure Rules, a "fast track" appeal must be lodged within 10 working days of the refusal (two working days if the applicant is at that time detained under Immigration Act powers), and must then be heard and determined within *seven* working days, compared with 42 days in standard, substantive appeals. Amnesty International has long argued that such a narrow time limit does not provide "fast track" appellants with an adequate opportunity to prepare their appeal.

In this respect it is important to note that, under the existing arrangements, the "fast track" mechanism is applied to cases where the issues in dispute at the appeal hearing are relatively limited. Currently, the vast majority of "fast track" appeals involve cases where the application has been summarily refused on "safe third country" grounds, ie without substantive examination of the merits of the asylum claim. In such cases the scope of the appeal is limited to whether the "third" country in question is indeed "safe" for the individual concerned; if the Special Adjudicator is not convinced that this is so, then he or she will refer the case back to the Home Office for substantive consideration of the merits of the asylum claim itself. Similarly, in those cases where the application has been refused on the grounds that it is "frivolous or vexatious", the principal issue in dispute is that of whether there is any substance at all to the asylum claim; in practice, where the Special Adjudicator is not convinced that the asylum claim is

---

4 Regrettably, it would seem that Ministers are unwilling to publish drafts of the new Procedural Rules until after the Bill has become law. This as yet unexplained delay in the publication of the new Procedural Rules has had the effect of hampering meaningful debate on Clause 1 of the Bill.

5 Under Paragraph 5(6) of Schedule 2 to the 1993 Act, the Special Adjudicator can, as an alternative to allowing or dismissing a "fast track" appeal, refer the case back to the Home Office for further consideration. It has been established through case law (*Mehari* [1994] Imm AR 151) that, in "safe third country" appeals, a Special Adjudicator who finds against the Home Office should refer the case back for substantive consideration under Paragraph 5(6), rather than allow the appeal outright. In those cases where the asylum application has been refused on the grounds that it is "frivolous or vexatious", however, a Special Adjudicator who finds against the Home Office (in that he or she is not convinced that there is no substance at all to the asylum claim) may either refer the case back to the Home Office under Paragraph 5(6) for further consideration, or allow the appeal outright.

simply "frivolous or vexatious", and that it therefore merits further substantive examination, then he or she is most likely to refer the case back to the Home Office for re-consideration, ie without going on to examine in full the *merits* of that asylum claim.**5**

Under the provisions of Clause 1, however, the "fast track" mechanism - with its narrow time limits - will cover *substantive* appeals where the issue in dispute is the far more complex one of whether the individual concerned does indeed have a well-founded fear of persecution in his or her country. Clearly, such substantive appeals require considerably greater preparation than those where the issues in dispute are relatively limited.

Furthermore, unlike the standard appeal procedure, the existing "fast track" appeal mechanism does not include a further right of appeal, on a point of law, to the Immigration Appeal Tribunal (IAT). It is of course inevitable that every Special Adjudicator will on occasion make an error of law when determining an asylum appeal, and the function of the IAT is to hear and determine counter appeals with a view to correcting such errors. In 1994, for example, the IAT determined 270 such counter appeals against a Special Adjudicator's dismissal of an asylum appeal, and 200 (74 per cent) of these counter appeals were either allowed or remitted back to another Special Adjudicator for re-hearing.**6** In other words, but for the existence of this further right of appeal to the IAT, 200 errors of law by Special Adjudicators would have gone uncorrected in 1994 alone. Moreover, the setting of legal precedent by the IAT (by means of such rulings) undoubtedly informs the subsequent decision-making of Special Adjudicators, thereby improving the quality of such decision-making. Amnesty International would therefore be deeply concerned if the new Procedural Rules were not to preserve the further right of appeal to the IAT (on a point of law) for cases covered by Clause 1 of the Bill.

Amnesty International is further concerned that the new Procedure Rules may contain provisions for some or all "fast track" appeals to be determined on the papers only, ie without an *oral* hearing. The abolition of oral appeal hearings in certain cases was one of the principal recommendations of the review carried out for the Home Office by KPMG Peat Marwick in late 1994, and ministers are known to be considering seriously the implementation of this recommendation. In Amnesty International's view, this would only further reduce the opportunities for those unjustly refused asylum to present effectively their response or counter-argument to the Home Office's reasons for refusal.

In this context, it must be noted that the terms of Clause 1 of the Bill are so wide-ranging that almost any rejected applicant may be subjected to the "fast track" appeals mechanism. Even if the applicant is not from one of the "designated" countries deemed not to produce refugees (see below), then his or

---

6 Source: Home Office Statistical Bulletin 15/95, Table 8.3.

her claim may be refused, and the appeal "fast tracked", on the grounds that - in the Home Office's view - the circumstances which gave rise to his or her fear of persecution "no longer subsist". This raises the prospect of asylum applicants from Bosnia and Rwanda, for example, being subjected to the "fast track" appeal mechanism following refusal of their asylum claim on the dubious grounds that the crisis which caused their flight has abated.

Alternatively, the appeal may be "fast tracked" on the grounds that the individual in question applied for asylum after being refused leave to enter the United Kingdom, or after entering the country without first gaining such leave (ie, illegally). However, those fleeing persecution may have valid reasons for applying for asylum after entering - or seeking to enter - the country on another basis or clandestinely, rather than immediately upon arrival. Having experienced repression first hand - and possibly still traumatised as a result - they may be fearful of authority and hopeful of seeking the advice and support of friends, relatives or refugee agencies before putting their fate in the hands of officialdom. Furthermore, the widespread imposition of visa regimes on refugee-producing countries, and their enforcement by the fining of carrier operators bringing those without a valid visa, has forced many would-be asylum-seekers to resort to the use of forged documents and/or clandestine means of travel (sometimes involving illegal means of entry). Clause 1 of the Bill raises the prospect of such applicants being subjected to the "fast track" appeals mechanism following refusal of their asylum claim, purely because of the manner of their entry, or attempted entry, to the United Kingdom - a factor which has no bearing on the legitimacy of their asylum claim.

Alternatively, the appeal may be "fast tracked" on the basis that, in the view of the Home Office, the applicant's fear of persecution - however genuine - is not "by reason of [his or her] race, religion, nationality, membership of a particular social group, or political opinion". This provision is significant because, at a meeting in Brussels on 23-24 November 1995, the European Union Justice & Home Affairs Council agreed a *Resolution on the Harmonised Application of the Refugee Definition, as set out in Article 1 of the [1951 UN Convention on Refugees]*. According to this Resolution, those fleeing persecution carried out by non-governmental agencies (eg armed opposition groups) will no longer qualify for asylum under Article 1 of the 1951 UN Convention. As the UN High Commissioner for Refugees (UNHCR) has stated, this "will allow States to avoid recognising as refugees people persecuted by non-state agents - such as rebel groups or extremist organisations. This creates an anomalous situation in which someone targeted by the Government in a civil conflict could gain asylum abroad, but not an equally innocent civilian persecuted by the opposition, as has been the case with many Algerians. If governmental authority

---

7 UNHCR press release, dated 24 November 1995.

collapses altogether - as has happened recently in Somalia and Liberia - no one might qualify for refugee status".7 Clause 1 of the Bill raises the prospect of such applicants being subjected to the "fast track" appeal mechanism following refusal of their asylum claim.

Perhaps the most controversial provision of Clause 1, however, is the application of the "fast track" appeal mechanism to cases of rejected applicants from a list of "designated" countries generally deemed not to produce refugees - the so-called "white list" mechanism already adopted in a number of European countries (eg Denmark, Finland, Germany, the Netherlands and Switzerland) and strongly recommended by the KPMG Peat Marwick study.

To date, the Home Secretary has announced a "white list" of seven countries - Bulgaria, Cyprus, Ghana, India, Pakistan, Poland and Romania - but a leaked Foreign Office memorandum confirms his intention of adding Ethiopia, Kenya and Tanzania - and almost certainly others, such as Nigeria - just as soon as the Bill has become law. Clause 1(4) of the Bill provides that an order by the Home Secretary to include a particular country on the "designated" list will be made by a Statutory Instrument tabled in either House of Parliament, and the Home Office has confirmed that the "designated" list is designed to be "flexible".

It is a fundamental principle of international refugee law that asylum applications must be determined *individually*, through a thorough examination of the circumstances of the person in question. The determination of whether persons would be at real risk of persecution in their own country is a difficult and complex process relying heavily on an evaluation of statements and claims (by the applicant) that are not always susceptible to proof, and on an objective assessment of the political and human rights situation in countries that are often undergoing complex and rapid change. Only a careful examination of each asylum-seeker's *individual* circumstances can exclude the possibility that he or she would be at risk on or after return, and ensure that the Government complies with its obligations under international law.

Although the Home Secretary has stated that all asylum claims by nationals of countries on the "white list" will continue to receive full, individual examination, there must be a risk that the mere existence of such a list will create a presumption in the minds of Home Office caseworkers that such asylum claims cannot be well-founded. Evidence of the risk of such a mentality developing has already been provided by a leaked Foreign Office memorandum on the "white list" mechanism, which states that asylum claims by nationals of countries on the list "are likely to be refused".8 Amnesty International is therefore concerned that, under this mechanism, an asylum claim by a national of a "white list" country will *not* receive a full, individualised examination, with an attendant

---

8 "Bigger white list tightens asylum rules", *The Guardian*, 8 February 1996.

increase in the risk of an unjust refusal. The appeal against this refusal will then be subject to the narrow time limits and other limitations of the "fast track" appeal mechanism, which offers an inadequate opportunity to challenge such unjust refusals.

In this context, Amnesty International is particularly concerned that a decision to include a particular country on the "white list" will be based upon inappropriate criteria. It is clear from the wording of the December 1992 EU Resolutions and Conclusions from which this measure originates, as well as the leaked Foreign Office memorandum referred to above and a Conservative Central Office briefing paper, that the primary consideration in any such decision will be the number of asylum-seekers arriving from that country and the proportion of *successful* applicants, rather than the human rights situation in that country.**9** Indeed, this would explain the inclusion of countries such as India, Kenya and Pakistan - countries where Amnesty International has documented widespread and serious human rights abuses - on the Home Office's initial "white list". It also suggests that it is only a matter of time before countries such as Algeria, Nigeria and Zaire - countries producing large numbers of asylum-seekers but with extremely low recognition rates - are added to the list.

Amnesty International is further concerned by the equivocal wording of Clause 1, which defines "white list" countries as those where "there is in general no serious risk of persecution". Human rights abuses are often targeted at particular ethnic, religious, political or other groups, and accordingly any notion of a "general" risk of persecution becomes meaningless when applied to many refugee-producing countries. As the Refugee Legal Centre has noted, Germany in 1936 could well have been designated as a country in which "there is in general no serious risk of persecution", because persecution by the Nazi authorities was directed at specific minority groups - eg Jews, homosexuals, gypsies, Communists - and the mass of the general population was not at risk. Moreover, as UNHCR has emphasised, "it is impossible to exclude, as a matter of law, the possibility that an individual could have a well-founded fear of persecution in any particular country, however great its attachment to human rights and the rule of law".**10**

Indeed, despite many positive developments in the political and human rights situation in countries such as Bulgaria, Ghana and Romania, it is clear that in each of these countries serious human rights abuses continue to be targeted at

---

9 For example, the Conservative Central Office briefing on the Bill, dated 21 February 1996, states that "any country on the list will need to meet three criteria: the country generates significant numbers of asylum applications; a very high proportion of applications from that country prove to be unfounded; and, in general, there is no serious risk of persecution."
10 *An overview of protection issues in Western Europe: Legislative trends and positions taken by UNHCR,* issued by the Regional Bureau for Europe of UNHCR, September 1995.

certain ethnic or social groups, as well as some political opponents. In Romania, for example, Amnesty International has documented the imprisonment of "prisoners of conscience" - in particular consenting adults engaging in homosexual acts in private - the torture and ill-treatment of detainees, suspicious deaths in police custody, and a nationwide pattern of police failure to protect the Roma minority from racist violence. In Amnesty International's view, the operation of the "white list" mechanism provided for by Clause 1 of the Bill would militate against the fair determination of asylum claims by individuals from such minority groups.

Clauses 2 and 3 of the Bill: the provisions

Currently, those applying for asylum having travelled to the United Kingdom not directly from the country of persecution, but via one or more transit countries, may be refused under the so-called "safe third country" rule (codified in Paragraphs 345 and 347 of the Immigration Rules). Under this rule, such applicants may be summarily refused - ie without any examination of the *substance* of their asylum claim - on the basis that they should have sought asylum in one of the transit countries they passed through. In general, the Home Office follows the common international practice - not sanctioned by international law -of seeking to return such applicants to the *last* transit country through which they passed before reaching the United Kingdom. In 1995, a total of 1,515 asylum applications were refused on this basis, representing just over seven per cent of all refusals.[11]

As described above, the Asylum & Immigration Appeals Act 1993 created a truncated and accelerated procedure for dealing with appeals in such cases. Although subject to narrow time limits on the lodging, hearing and determination of appeals, this mechanism provides all such appellants with an oral hearing before an IAA Special Adjudicator. It has been established through case law that the function of the Special Adjudicator in such appeals is to independently examine the question of whether the "third country" in question is "safe" *for the individual concerned,* and that the burden of proof lies with the Home Office. The same case law also established, in October 1993, that if the Special Adjudicator is not convinced that the "third country" is indeed "safe" for the individual concerned, then he or she should refer the case back to the Home Office for substantive consideration of the merits of the asylum claim itself - a mechanism provided for by Paragraph 5(6) of Schedule 2 to the 1993 Act - rather than allowing the appeal outright.[12]

In line with the June 1995 European Union *Resolution on Minimum Guarantees for Asylum Procedures,* Clause 2 of the Bill provides that an asylum applicant

---

11 Source: *Hansard* (House of Commons), 8 February 1996, col. 309 (written answer).
12 *R. v Special Adjudicators, ex parte Mehari and others,* [1994] Imm AR 151.

who has been refused on "safe third country" grounds cannot appeal against that refusal prior to "being removed from, or being required to leave" the UK.**13** Clause 3 of the Bill creates a new right to appeal, *exercisable from outside the UK only*, on the ground that the Home Office "acted unreasonably" in refusing the asylum application on "safe third country" grounds. In short, Clauses 2 and 3 effectively abolish the right to appeal *prior to expulsion* in any case where the asylum application has been refused on "safe third country" grounds.

In January 1996, the Government announced an amendment to the Bill which would limit the scope of Clauses 2 and 3 to those cases where the "third country" in question is a member state of the European Union.**14** However, an analysis of 736 "safe third country" appeals determined in the 17-month period August 1994 -December 1995, carried out by the Refugee Legal Centre and published in January 1996, shows that the "third country" in question is an EU member state in some 93 per cent of such cases. Indeed, the Government has itself stated that the "third country" in question is an EU member state in "more than 95 per cent of cases".**15** In other words, this apparent concession would benefit only a very small proportion of all "safe third country" cases.

Clauses 2 and 3: Amnesty International's concerns

The first thing that has to be said about these two clauses is that, for the overwhelming majority of such cases, they abolish a legal safeguard that - notwithstanding its obvious shortcomings - has proven to be extremely valuable in practice. For it is clear that, since its creation in July 1993, the appeal mechanism in "safe third country" cases has provided vital protection to a very large proportion of those refused on "safe third country" grounds by the Home Office.

For example, a study of 60 asylum-seekers (selected at random) refused on "safe third country" grounds in the period 1 September 1994 - 31 March 1995, carried out by Amnesty International and published in June 1995, revealed a 43.3 per cent success rate at appeal.**16** More recently, an analysis of 419 "safe third

---

13 Paragraph 22 of the EU *Resolution on Minimum Guarantees for Asylum Procedures* (June 1995) states that, in such cases, there can be a derogation from the "general principle" (set out in Paragraph 17) that those refused asylum be allowed to remain in the country until such time as their appeal has been heard and determined; it also states that, in such cases, the reasons for the refusal of asylum can be communicated "orally instead of in writing".

14 *Hansard* (Standing Committee D on the Asylum & Immigration Bill), 23 January 1996, col. 257 (Timothy Kirkhope MP). However, in announcing this provision, ministers have added that its scope may in due course be revised to encompass countries such as "Switzerland, Canada and the USA", as well as the EU member states (ie Austria, Belgium, Denmark, Finland, France, Germany, Greece, Ireland, Italy, Luxembourg, Netherlands, Portugal, Spain and Sweden). This amendment was formally tabled during the Bill's Report Stage in the House of Commons on 21 February 1996.

15 *Hansard* (House of Commons), 21 February 1996, col. 445 (Ann Widdecombe MP).

16 See *Playing Human Pinball: Home Office practice in "safe third country" asylum cases* (June 1995). Of the 60 cases in this study, the appeal was referred back to the Home Office, under Paragraph 5(6), for substantive consideration in 23 cases, and the appeal was conceded by the Home Office in a further three cases.

country" appeals determined in the nine-month period 1 January - 11 October 1995, undertaken by the London office of the UN High Commissioner for Refugees (UNHCR), has demonstrated a 41.8 per cent success rate.**17**

Similarly, an analysis of 517 "safe third country" appeals determined in the 10-month period November 1994 - August 1995, undertaken by the Immigration Law Practitioners' Association (ILPA) and published in November 1995, demonstrated a 41.7 per cent success rate.**18** And an analysis of 736 "safe third country" appeals determined in the 17-month period August 1994 -December 1995, undertaken by the Refugee Legal Centre and published in January 1996, demonstrated a 38.7 per cent success rate.**19** Of course, such a high proportion of successful appeals not only underscores the considerable value of this legal safeguard, but casts serious doubt on the integrity of the Home Office's initial decision-making in such cases.

Moreover, it is clear that, even where the appeal to the IAA is dismissed, in a significant proportion of cases the Home Office subsequently rescinds its decision to refuse the application on "safe third country" grounds - and admits the application to the full procedure for substantive consideration - due to a successful application to the High Court for judicial review of the Special Adjudicator's determination. Of the 60 "safe third country" cases monitored by Amnesty International in late 1994 and early 1995, for example, the appeal was successful in 26 cases (43.3 per cent). But in a further 11 cases (18.3 per cent), the Home Office eventually agreed to consider the application substantively, despite the appeal having been dismissed by the IAA, following an application to the High Court for judicial review. Indeed, to date, the Home Office has rescinded its original decision and agreed to consider the asylum application substantively in 51 out of these 60 cases (85 per cent), while a further six cases remain unresolved many months after the date of the original application.

In this context it is important to note that the "third country" in question is an EU member state in the overwhelming majority of those cases where the appeal is *successful*. Of the 175 successful appeals recorded by UNHCR between 1 January - 11 October 1995, the "third country" in question was an EU member state in 166 cases (94.8 per cent). Of the 28 appeals where Italy was the "third

---

17 Of the total of 419 "safe third country" appeal determinations received by UNHCR (which is a party to all such appeals) in this period, the case had been referred back to the Home Office, under Paragraph 5(6), for substantive consideration in 175 cases. This analysis also demonstrated that the "safe third country" in question was an EU member state in 94.5 per cent of these 419 appeals.

18 *Summaries of Special Adjudicators Decisions, No. 2*, ILPA, November 1995. Of the 517 "safe third country" appeal determinations examined by ILPA, the case had been referred back to the Home Office, under Paragraph 5(6), for substantive consideration in 216 cases. This sample of 517 "safe third country" appeals undoubtedly represents the overwhelming majority of such appeals determined during this 10-month period.

19 RLC press release, dated 22 January 1996. Of the 736 "safe third country" appeal determinations examined by the RLC, the case had been referred back to the Home Office, under Paragraph 5(6), for substantive consideration in 285 cases. This sample of 736 "safe third country" appeals undoubtedly represents the overwhelming majority of such appeals determined during this 17-month period.

country" in question, for example, the appeal was successful in 23 cases (82 per cent), while in all nine cases where the "third country" in question was Portugal the appeal was successful. Similarly, of the total of 285 successful appeals recorded by the Refugee Legal Centre in the 17-month period August 1994 - December 1995, the "third country" in question was an EU member state in 250 cases (87.7 per cent). Of the 115 cases where Belgium was the "third country" in question, for example, the appeal was successful in 62 cases (53.9 per cent).

In seeking to justify Clauses 2 and 3, Ministers have argued that a right of appeal *prior to expulsion* is unnecessary in such cases because, in their words, "it is reasonable to assume that our European neighbours are safe countries".[20] But this argument overlooks the cardinal rule of refugee protection, which is that each and every case must be examined on an *individual* basis, in order to take account of the particular circumstances leading to the making of the asylum application. The issue in dispute at "safe third country" appeals is not so much that of whether France, or Germany or Italy is, in general terms, "unsafe" for all asylum-seekers (although, in the case of some countries, it may be clear that this is so). Rather, the issue in dispute is that of whether the country in question is "safe" *for the individual concerned*, in that he or she will be re-admitted to that country *and* will have there an effective opportunity to seek and, if appropriate, obtain asylum.

It is clear from the above figures that, since July 1993, IAA Special Adjudicators have ruled in a very large proportion of cases - including many cases where the "third country" in question is an EU member state - that there can be no confidence that these two conditions will be met if the individual concerned is expelled to that "third country". For example, among the 419 "safe third country" appeals recorded by UNHCR between 1 January and 11 October 1995, France was the "third country" in 174 cases. While the appeal was dismissed in 117 of these cases, in 57 cases the application was referred back to the Home Office, under Paragraph 5(6) of Schedule 2 to the 1993 Act, for substantive consideration. Presumably, in the particular circumstances of these 57 cases the Special Adjudicator decided that there could be no guarantee that the individual concerned would be readmitted to France *and* would have there an effective opportunity to seek asylum.

However, in seeking to justify Clauses 2 and 3, ministers -including the Home Secretary - have gone to great lengths to hide or obscure the true value of this right to appeal. During the Second Reading debate on the Bill in the House of Commons, on 11 December 1995, Mr Howard sought to sweep objections aside by falsely claiming that the success rate among such "safe third country" appeals

---

20 *Hansard* (Standing Committee D on the Asylum & Immigration Bill), 25 January 1996, col. 339 (Timothy Kirkhope MP).

is a mere "four per cent".**21** This attempt to diminish the value of what is clearly an essential legal safeguard was subsequently repeated by Mr Howard's junior ministers, Ann Widdecombe MP and Timothy Kirkhope MP, in sessions of the House of Commons Standing Committee on the Bill.

In making this false claim, ministers appear to be relying in part on the figures set out in Table 8.4 of Home Office Statistical Bulletin 15/95, *Asylum Statistics United Kingdom 1994*. This shows that, of the total of 530 "fast track" appeals determined by IAA Special Adjudicators in 1994, four per cent were "allowed". However, ministers appear to have overlooked the fact that, according to Table 8.4 of the Statistical Bulletin, in a further 26 per cent of these 530 appeals the case was referred back to the Home Office under Paragraph 5(6) of Schedule 2 to the 1993 Act. And, as described above, such a referral is the appropriate action in any "safe third country" appeal where the Special Adjudicator finds against the Home Office - that is, where the appeal is successful. In other words, even according to the Home Office's own figures, the success rate among *all* "fast track" appeals in 1994 was at least 30 per cent. More recently, the Home Office has also confirmed that, of the 1,115 "fast track" appeals determined in 1995, three per cent were allowed and 29 per cent were referred back under Paragraph 5(6); in other words, the success rate among *all* "fast track" appeals in 1995 was at least 32 per cent.**22**

Furthermore, ministers appear also to have overlooked the fact that a significant proportion of "fast track" appeals are not fully determined because they are *withdrawn*, and in the overwhelming majority of such cases that is due to the Home Office conceding the issues in dispute shortly before the appeal hearing. In "safe third country" cases, the legal and practical consequences of such action by the Home Office are exactly the same as if the appeal had been heard and the case referred back under Paragraph 5(6) - ie the case will then be substantively examined. According to Table 8.4 of Home Office Statistical Bulletin 15/95, in 1994 six per cent of all "fast track" appeals were withdrawn, and more recently ministers have confirmed that in 1995 nine per cent of all "fast track" appeals were withdrawn.**23** If these figures are added to the Home Office's own figures for "fast track" appeals that have either been allowed or referred back under Paragraph 5(6), then the total proportion of successful "fast track" appeals was 36 per cent in 1994, and 41 per cent in 1995 - figures not dissimilar to those demonstrated by the research of Amnesty International, UNHCR, ILPA and the Refugee Legal Centre.

However, it must also be noted that these Home Office figures relate to *all* "fast track" appeals - ie, those where the asylum claim has been refused as "frivolous

---

21 *Hansard* (House of Commons), 11 December 1995, col.705.
22 *Hansard* (House of Commons), 8 February 1995, col. 308 (written answer).
23 *Ibid.*

or vexatious", as well as those where the asylum claim has been refused on "safe third country" grounds - and all the information available suggests that the success rate at appeal in "frivolous and vexatious" cases is somewhat lower than that in "safe third country" cases. For example, in the nine-month period 1 January - 11 October 1995, the London office of UNHCR recorded a success rate at appeal of 29 per cent in "frivolous and vexatious" cases, compared to a success rate at appeal of 41.8 per cent in "safe third country" cases. Accordingly, the *average* success rate indicated by the Home Office figures is lower than the actual success rate in "safe third country" appeals. In short, if all these factors are taken into account, the Home Office's own figures support the research findings of Amnesty International, UNHCR, ILPA and the Refugee Legal Centre.

It has long been demonstrated, by Amnesty International and others, that application of the so-called "safe third country" rule, without proper safeguards, carries a substantial risk of asylum-seekers being expelled to *unsafe* third countries where, instead of being admitted to a satisfactory asylum procedure, they may be expelled to the country from which they have fled and where they face persecution.[24] It has also been demonstrated that such practice carries a risk of asylum-seekers being successively expelled (on "safe third country" grounds) from one transit country to another, or of them being left "in orbit" between two or more countries unwilling to accept responsibility for dealing with their asylum claim. (All western European countries now apply the "safe third country" rule, and most operate accelerated procedures - with minimal or non-existent appeal rights - in such cases). Such "chain removals" and "orbit" situations may ultimately result in asylum-seekers being returned to transit countries - eg some of those in eastern Europe, the Middle East and Asia - where the asylum procedures are seriously deficient or non-existent, and where they may therefore be unable to obtain effective protection and may face expulsion to the country of persecution.

It is difficult to envisage how an asylum-seeker who has been "chain removed" from the United Kingdom, to France, to Germany, to Latvia and then to Russia, say, would be able to pursue an appeal against the Home Office's refusal from Russia, where there is no legal provision for asylum-seekers. The abolition of the right of appeal *prior to expulsion* in such cases, therefore, would only increase the risk of such breaches of the 1951 UN Convention on Refugees and other international law. And the Government cannot claim to be complying with its obligations under international law while taking steps which have the effect, if not the intention, of leading directly to breaches of such international law.

---

[24] See, for example, *Playing Human Pinball: Home Office practice in "safe third country" asylum cases*, Amnesty International UK (June 1995); and *Safe third countries: myths and realities*, European Council on Refugees & Exiles (February 1995).

In this respect, it should be noted that these provisions of the Bill are in contravention of international standards for the protection of refugees. The inter-governmental Executive Committee of the UN High Commission for Refugees (UNHCR) has explicitly stated that a rejected asylum-seeker should be permitted to remain in the country while an appeal (to a higher administrative authority or to the courts) is pending.**25** UNHCR has further stated that there can be "no exceptions" to this principle.

In this context, it should be noted that the implementation of Clauses 2 and 3 would result in the "safe third country" rule being applied to far greater numbers of port applicants than at present. Indeed, Amnesty International believes that the overwhelming majority of port applicants could be affected by this measure.

In 1995, there were over 14,400 "port" applicants (representing 33 per cent of all applicants), but only 1,300 were refused on "safe third country" grounds.**26** And yet there can be little doubt that a significant proportion - if not the vast majority - of these 14,400 port applicants arrived at the United Kingdom's borders not directly from the country of persecution, but via one or more transit countries. It would seem that it is only the existence of the appeal mechanism established by the 1993 Act that has prevented the Home Office applying the "safe third country" rule to far greater numbers of port applicants. In short, the existing "fast track" appeal mechanism simply could not cope with significantly greater numbers of such refusals. With the abolition of the right of appeal for the overwhelming majority of such applicants, however, this limitation on application of the "safe third country" rule would no longer apply.

In other words, the implementation of Clauses 2 and 3 of the Bill could result in the "safe third country" rule being applied to many - perhaps most - of those who apply for asylum immediately upon arrival at a port, ie the one group of asylum-seekers retaining entitlement to benefits under the Social Security Regulations which came into force on 5 February 1996. And, in practice, this would result in the refusal and expulsion of such applicants within minutes or hours of their arrival at an airport or seaport. In short, most such applicants would be unlikely to get past the immigration desk at Heathrow, Dover or Waterloo, let alone set foot in any DSS office to claim Social Security benefits.

---

25 UNHCR Executive Committee Conclusion 8 ("Determination of refugee status") and Conclusion 30 ("The problem of manifestly unfounded or abusive applications for refugee status or asylum"). Since 1975 the Executive Committee of UNHCR has adopted a number of *Conclusions on the International Protection of Refugees,* setting out a number of basic requirements which States' asylum procedures should satisfy. Under Article 35 of the 1951 UN Convention on Refugees, contracting states undertake to "cooperate" with UNHCR and "shall in particular facilitate its duty of supervising the application of the Convention". **26** Source: *Hansard* (House of Commons), 8 February 1996, col. 309 (written answer).

The context: further background information

Introduction

In seeking to justify the introduction of the new Social Security regulations and the Asylum & Immigration Bill, ministers and others have resorted to a number of different arguments relating to the current pattern of asylum applications. In particular, ministers have placed great emphasis on the significant increase in the number of applications for asylum in the United Kingdom since the late 1980s, and the relatively small proportion of applicants ultimately granted asylum.

In doing so, ministers have clearly sought to imply that the majority of asylum applicants are "bogus refugees" seeking to circumvent the United Kingdom's immigration controls (or avoid deportation) for economic reasons.

In Amnesty International's view, this simplistic and emotive reasoning is seriously flawed. Not only does it fail to take proper account of the current unprecedented levels of governmental oppression and conflict leading to refugee movements, but it glosses over the manifest failings of the existing asylum process. As the United Nations High Commissioner for Refugees (UNHCR) has emphasised: "a country's recognition rate of refugees may more often reflect the narrowness or liberalness of that State's application of the refugee definition than the legitimacy or otherwise of individual claims".[1]

The number of asylum applications

There has indeed been a significant increase in the number of people seeking asylum in the United Kingdom since the late 1980s. Whereas there were some 4,000 asylum applications in 1988, for example, there were 32,800 applications in 1994 and 43,965 applications in 1995. While there are almost certainly a number of complex factors behind this increase, it is clear that much of the increase can be linked to a deterioration of the human rights situation in certain countries, the most obvious examples being:

The former Yugoslavia, up from just nine asylum applications in 1988, reaching a peak of 5,635 applications in 1992 and then (largely due to the imposition of a visa regime on Yugoslav nationals in late 1992) down to 1,385 applications in 1994, and 1,565 in 1995;

Algeria (where a spiral of political violence since the imposition of a state of emergency in February 1992 has claimed over 50,000 lives): up from just 20 asylum applications in 1990, to 995 applications in 1994, and 1,965 in 1995;

Nigeria (where there has been a serious deterioration in the human rights

---

1 Representations to the SSAC by the London office of UNHCR, November 1995.

situation since a military coup in November 1993): up from just 10 asylum applications in 1988, to 4,340 applications in 1994, and 5,825 in 1995;

Somalia (where the fall of the Barre regime in January 1991 led to what the UN has described as the "worst humanitarian disaster in the world"): up from 305 asylum applications in 1988, to 1,840 applications in 1994, and 3,465 in 1995; and

Kenya (whose deteriorating human rights record has come under growing international criticism): up from just four asylum applications in 1988, to 1,130 applications in 1994, and 1,385 in 1995.

Asylum applications by nationals of these *five* countries alone accounted for one third of all applications in 1995. Such figures suggest that the increase in the number of asylum applications since 1988 is closely associated with the unprecedented levels of political terror, oppression and armed conflict found not only in these countries, but also in countries such as Afghanistan, China, Colombia, India, Iran, Iraq, Sri Lanka, Sudan, Turkey and Zaire.

However, perhaps the most important point to make about the number of applicants is that the Government has a legal obligation to offer protection to genuine refugees, and therefore to operate a fair and satisfactory asylum-determination process, *whatever the number of applicants.* There is nothing in the 1951 UN Convention that would imply that a government's obligations cease once the number of asylum applications rises above a certain level. In other words, a rise in the number of applicants - whatever its causes - cannot justify the erosion or removal of essential legal safeguards, let alone the effective dismantling of the entire process.

The Home Office's recognition rates

The Home Office's overall recognition rates are indeed very low. Of the total of 20,990 initial decisions made by the Asylum Division in 1994, asylum was granted in 825 cases (3.9 per cent) and Exceptional Leave to Remain (ELR) was granted in 3,660 cases (17.4 per cent).**2** And of the total of 27,005 initial decisions made in 1995, asylum was granted in 1,295 cases (4.7 per cent) and ELR was granted in 4,410 cases (16.3 (per cent).**3**

There are a number of things that can be said about these recognition rates. The

---

2 ELR is granted in those cases where the Home Office is not satisfied that the applicant qualifies for asylum, but accepts that there are strong "humanitarian or compassionate" reasons why the applicant should be allowed to remain in the UK. Whereas asylum is granted for a period of four years (after which indefinite leave to remain may be applied for), ELR is granted for 12 months initially and then (subject to renewal) for two further periods of three years (after which indefinite leave to remain may be applied for). Unlike those granted asylum, applicants granted ELR have no right to family reunion.
3 Sources: Home Office Statistical Bulletin 15/95; and *Hansard* (House of Commons), 8 February 1996, col. 307 (written answer).

first is that, despite no apparent change in the nature or quality of genuine asylum claims, the overall recognition rate (ie the proportion of cases determined in which either asylum or ELR is granted) has fallen substantially since 1990 (when asylum was granted in 22.8 per cent of cases determined and ELR was granted in 59.6 per cent). This is undoubtedly due in large part to a much more restrictive approach to individual cases from 1991 onwards - eventually codified in the Immigration Rules accompanying the 1993 Act - and the associated growth of a "culture of disbelief" in the Home Office's Asylum Division.

Paragraphs 340 - 344 of the Immigration Rules (HC 395) set out a number of tendentious criteria which "may damage an asylum applicant's credibility" and "lead to refusal". These include: "a failure to make a prompt and full disclosure of material factors"; a failure to "apply [for asylum] forthwith upon arrival in the UK"; the destruction, damage or disposal "of any passport, other document or ticket"; and that (in the Home Office's view) the applicant could or should have gone to another part of his or her own country to escape persecution. These factors are frequently cited in Home Office refusal letters as reasons for doubting the credibility of the applicant, and therefore for rejecting the application. However, as the United Nations High Commissioner for Refugees noted at the time the Rules were first issued, "evaluation of credibility is a process which involves the consideration of many complex factors, both objective and subjective, which are impossible to enumerate. Since all these may be equally important, singling out any of these factors will, by necessity, be incomplete and arbitrary".4 Indeed, in Amnesty International's view, these Rules are designed to facilitate the *refusal* of an asylum application, rather than a full and proper consideration of the individualised circumstances of the claim.

This narrow approach to the examination of individual asylum claims is frequently compounded by a flawed assessment of the human rights situation in the country in question. For example, until December 1995 the current Home Office country profile on Nigeria advised Asylum Division caseworkers that there was "no evidence that Ogonis ... face persecution from the Nigerian authorities for membership of MOSOP [the Movement for the Survival of the Ogoni People]".

And yet since February 1995 Ken Saro-Wiwa and eight other members of MOSOP - an organisation which has been repeatedly targeted by the Nigerian authorities in recent years because of its political campaign against environmental damage in Ogoniland and for increased autonomy for the Ogoni ethnic group - had been facing politically-motivated charges in a blatantly and grossly

---

4 *UNHCR's observations to the Asylum Bill and related Rules,* issued by the London office of UNHCR in November 1992.

unfair trial. On 30 and 31 October 1995 the nine defendants were convicted and sentenced to death, and on 10 November all nine were executed. Not only had this trial been widely reported, amid international condemnation of the Nigerian authorities, but an Amnesty International report published (and sent to the Home Office) in July 1995 had described widespread "extrajudicial executions by the security forces and mass arrests" of members and supporters of MOSOP during 1993 and 1994. The same report described the detention of journalists, human rights activists, students, pro-democracy activists, environmental observers and others, as well as the ill-treatment of detainees and the banning of newspapers and trade unions. Given the existence of such a flawed Home Office "country profile", it is hardly surprising that, in the first ten months of 1995, only two Nigerians were granted asylum by Asylum Division caseworkers.

However, the Asylum Division's recognition rates also suggest that, since July 1993, the Home Office has operated an unofficial and undisclosed quota system, whereby the total number of applicants granted *either* asylum or ELR is kept below an arbitrary ceiling of approximately 20 per cent of all decisions made. In the second half of 1993, the proportion of applicants granted either asylum or ELR was 23 per cent, in the first half of 1994 it was 22 per cent, in the second half of 1994 it was 21 per cent, and in 1995 it was 21 per cent.5 Such uniformity is hardly what one would expect, and indeed very different to the situation pre-July 1993, when total recognition rates varied enormously over time (eg, from 82.4 per cent in 1990, to 44.4 per cent in 1991, and 64.6 per cent in the first half of 1993).

Furthermore, it would appear that there is a quota within the quota: in each of these time periods since July 1993 the number of applicants granted asylum has been approximately 20 per cent of all those granted either asylum or ELR. In other words, the Home Office Asylum Division appears to be operating to the following formula: only 20 per cent of applicants can be granted asylum or ELR (with the remaining 80 per cent being refused outright), and of these only 20 per cent can be granted asylum.

In short, it is Amnesty International's view that the current low recognition rates reflect the narrowness of the Home Office's application of the refugee definition (as set out in Article 1 of the 1951 UN Convention on Refugees), and the imposition of an arbitrary ceiling on the granting of asylum and ELR, rather than the legitimacy or otherwise of individual asylum claims. Accordingly, it would be entirely wrong to assume that such low recognition rates are in themselves indicative of widespread "misuse" of the asylum process by those

---

5 Sources: Home Office Statistical Bulletins 17/94 and 15/95; and *Hansard* (House of Commons), 8 February 1996, col. 307 (written answer).

merely seeking to circumvent the United Kingdom's immigration controls, as government ministers and others have repeatedly claimed.

With regard to appeals, the experience of refugee agencies and other legal representatives suggests that Immigration Appeal Authority (IAA) Special Adjudicators have not themselves adjusted to this change in Home Office recognition rates. Some of the current Special Adjudicators have been in post since the 1980s, when as many as 80 per cent of applicants were granted asylum or ELR. Because the initial recognition rate was so high, it was rare for a good case to have to go to appeal, and accordingly there were very few successful appeals. As a result, IAA Adjudicators developed a highly sceptical view of appellants, and it would seem that some retain this mind set. And, of course, new Special Adjudicators have been trained by their longer-serving colleagues.

However, it is also important to note that, in claiming that "only four per cent of appeals to [the IAA] adjudicators actually succeed"[6], ministers overlook the fact that a significant proportion of asylum appeals to the IAA are not determined because they are *withdrawn* by the appellant, and in the overwhelming majority of such cases this is due to the Home Office conceding the issues in dispute some time before the appeal hearing. And, of course, in conceding the issues in dispute the Home Office is in effect conceding that the original decision was unjust. According to the Home Office's own figures, in 1994 some four per cent of all substantive asylum appeals were allowed, while a further 11 per cent were withdrawn. And in 1995, while three per cent of all substantive asylum appeals were allowed, a further 16 per cent were withdrawn.[7]

The most important point to make about the Home Office and IAA recognition rates, however, is that low recognition rates do not in themselves justify the erosion or removal of essential legal safeguards, let alone the effective dismantling of the entire asylum process. The Home Office has - over a period of several years - taken steps to ensure that recognition rates are low; it then cites these artificially low recognition rates as the justification for tightening the system even more, by disabling or removing essential safeguards - a process which may of course lead to even lower recognition rates. As the United Nations High Commissioner for Refugees (UNHCR) has noted, "there are many dangers in such a self-justificatory and circular analysis".[8] The fact of the matter is that, under international law, it doesn't matter how low the overall recognition rate is - the Government still has a legal obligation to protect genuine refugees and that requires the existence of a fair, effective and satisfactory asylum-determination procedure.

---

6 *Hansard* (House of Commons), 11 December 1995, col. 700 (Mr Michael Howard).
7 Sources: Home Office Statistical Bulletin 15/95, Tables 8.3 & 8.4; and *Hansard* (House of Commons), 20 February 1996, col. 103 (written answer).
8 *Certain comments by the United Nations High Commissioner for Refugees on the Asylum & Immigration Bill 1995*, issued by the London office of UNHCR in January 1996.

Delays in the process

In 1993, Home Office ministers and officials stated that the Asylum & Immigration Appeals Act would remove delays in the asylum process, by providing for "prompt and fair" decisions. Indeed, during its passage through Parliament, ministers confidently predicted that the Act would result in asylum cases being fully resolved (ie including any appeal) "within three months".[9] However, according to the Government' own figures, it is now taking an average of 18.7 months.[10]

This failure to meet the targets set out in 1993 is due largely to continuing inefficiency and poor productivity within the Home Office. Contrary to the predictions of ministers and officials in 1993, that initial decisions would be taken within a "maximum" of 28 days,[11] the Asylum Division is currently taking an average of 8.9 months to make an initial decision.[12] It is then taking an average of 3.7 months to process appeals (ie, prepare its response to the lodging of the appeal and send the appeal papers to the IAA). There can be little doubt that two significant factors contributing to such excessive delays are the minimal amount of computerisation within the Asylum Division and the retention of outdated and highly inefficient working practices. For example, in many cases the interview of the applicant and the consideration of the results of that interview are carried out by two separate officials, thereby involving much unnecessary duplication of work and transfer of files. And the Asylum Division structure involves considerable demarcation of staff functions, thereby involving further time-consuming transfer of files between caseworkers, typists and others. Given the retention of such inefficient working practices, it is perhaps not surprising that the backlog of outstanding asylum applications has grown steadily, from 46,300 in July 1993 to 69,650 on 31 December 1995.[13]

Furthermore, this failure on the part of the Home Office Asylum Division to meet the targets for decision times set out by ministers in 1993 has occurred despite substantial increases in staff resources. Indeed, the Government has stated that there are now "almost 800" staff working on asylum cases, compared

---

9 The then Home Secretary, Kenneth Clarke MP, speaking during the Second Reading of the Asylum & Immigration Appeals Bill, *Hansard* (House of Commons), 2 November 1992, col. 32.
10 Source: *Hansard* (House of Commons), 8 February 1996, col. 310 (written answer).
11 A Home Office explanatory note, issued in October 1992 for the Second Reading of the Asylum & Immigration Appeals Bill, states that "some" initial decisions would be made "within hours or a few days", and that all decisions would be made within "28 days". The note also states that "all time limits are maxima in normal circumstances".
12 Source: *Hansard*, (House of Commons), 8 February 1996, col. 310 (written answer). It should be noted that new applications receive priority over applications submitted prior to the implementation of the 1993 Act and still outstanding. According to the same written answer, the average time currently taken by the Asylum Division to reach an initial decision on applications submitted pre-July 1993 is 40.0 months (ie more than three years).
13 Sources: *Hansard* (House of Commons), 21 July 1993, col. 208; and 8 February 1996, col. 310 (written answers).

with "fewer than 100 in 1988".[14] Despite this substantial increase in staff resources, the number of decisions made by the Asylum Division fell from 34,900 in 1992, to 23,500 in 1993 and 21,000 in 1994, while in 1995 the rate of decision-making picked up only slightly, with 27,005 decisions. So productivity has fallen significantly, while the number of applications has risen. Moreover, this fall in productivity has occurred despite the simplification of the initial decision-making process arising from the implementation of the 1993 Act. The creation of a universal right of appeal (with suspensive effect on removal) under the 1993 Act enabled the Home Office to dispense with the time-consuming "minded to refuse" procedure, whereby the applicant's legal representative was given an opportunity to challenge the Asylum Division's preliminary assessment of the claim prior to a formal refusal.

In addition, there is clearly an under-resourcing of the asylum appeals system. In short, there are simply not enough Special Adjudicators to cope adequately with the number of refusals being made by the Home Office. As a result, the IAA currently takes an average of 6.1 months to determine an asylum appeal, instead of the predicted *maximum* of nine weeks.[15] Accordingly, the backlog of asylum appeals awaiting determination by the IAA has grown steadily, to 4,885 on 31 May 1995, and 11,690 on 31 December 1995.[16]

But another factor in this failure to meet the 1993 targets is the complexity of much of the process. Perhaps the best example of this is the "fast track" appeal system for so-called "safe third country" cases, ie those where the applicant arrives at the United Kingdom's borders not directly from the country of persecution, but via one or more transit (or "third") countries. A key provision of the 1993 Act, this was supposed to act as a rapid "screening out" mechanism, thereby avoiding the need to deal with such cases substantively. At the time, the then Home Secretary, Kenneth Clarke MP, confidently predicted that such cases would be fully resolved "within a week to 10 days", thus freeing resources for substantive cases.[17]

However, research carried out by Amnesty International and published in June 1995 demonstrates that this procedure has proven to be neither rapid nor productive in terms of removals to "third countries". Not only have the Home

---

14 *Hansard* (House of Commons), 22 February 1996, col. 543 (Michael Howard MP).
15 The Asylum Appeals (Procedure) Rules 1993, which accompany the 1993 Act, set out strict time limits for the lodging, hearing and determination of appeals. Under the Rules, substantive appeals must be lodged within 10 working days of the Home Office's refusal of the asylum claim; and the appeal hearing must be completed, including any necessary adjournments, within 42 days (ie six weeks) of the appeal being lodged. A Home Office explanatory note, issued in October 1992, states that "all time limits are maxima in normal circumstances and many cases will be resolved more quickly ... initial decisions and appeals to the adjudicator will be completed within three months".
16 Sources: *Hansard* (House of Commons), 20 June 1995, col. 137; and 8 February 1996, col. 310.
17 *Hansard* (House of Commons), 2 November 1992, col. 32.

Office and the IAA proven to be incapable of dealing with "fast track" cases within anywhere near the time-scale envisaged by ministers and prescribed in the Asylum Appeals (Procedure) Rules 1993 - with the result that on average it takes some three months to resolve such cases - but, as predicted by Amnesty International and others in 1992, the efficacy of the process as a whole has been seriously compromised by its inherent unfairness and, accordingly, its suscepti-bility to challenges in the High Court by way of judicial review. Moreover, a significant factor in the preponderance of judicial review applications is the fact that the "fast track" appeals procedure has - to a large extent - become an "asylum lottery", with inconsistent decision-making by IAA Special Adjudica-tors in respect of whether particular transit countries can be considered "safe" for the individuals concerned. For these and other reasons, the net result is that, in some 85 per cent or more of cases *where the applicant is legally represented*, the Home Office is ultimately obliged to rescind its original decision and admit the asylum claim to the full procedure for substantive determination.**18**

In short, the efficacy of the existing "fast track" mechanism has been seriously compromised by the poor quality of much of the Home Office's decision-making, the failure of the Home Office and IAA to meet the prescribed time limits, and the mechanism's susceptibility to challenges in the High Court by way of judicial review. There seems to be little reason for thinking that the greatly extended "fast track" mechanism provided for in Clause 1 of the Bill would prove to be any more efficacious.

The "fast tracking" of applicants from the "white list" of supposedly "safe" countries of origin, for example, would almost certainly result in a proliferation of applications to the High Court for judicial review of the Home Office decision, leading to further delays and backlogs. And the more controversial the countries on the list - such as India, Kenya, Nigeria and Sri Lanka - the more judicial review applications there are likely to be. Accordingly, it is quite possible that the "white list" mechanism - intended to act as a rapid "screening out" of unfounded claims - would make little if any impact on overall decision times and backlogs.

The problem of "misuse" of the asylum process

It is not disputed that misuse or "abuse" of the asylum process by those merely

---

18 For further information, see *Playing human pinball: Home Office practice in "safe third country" asylum cases*, Amnesty International UK (June 1995), and also *The Asylum and Immigration Bill* above. Of the 60 "safe third country" cases monitored by Amnesty International during this nine-month study, the appeal to the IAA was successful in 23 cases, and the Home Office conceded the appeal in a further three cases. In addition, the Home Office agreed to consider the claim substantively in a further 11 cases following an application for judicial review; in three cases following the "bouncing back" of the individual from the "third country" in question; and in a further 11 cases for other reasons. At the time of writing, a further six cases remain unresolved. Only one applicant was permanently removed from the United Kingdom, while two applicants made a voluntary departure.

seeking to circumvent general immigration controls (or avoid deportation) is a significant and difficult problem for many European governments, and it is not in question that *some* of the recent increase in the number of asylum applications in the United Kingdom can be attributed to this wholly undesirable phenomenon. However, it should be noted that, to date, the Government has failed to provide any credible evidence of the *extent* of such misuse or "abuse" of the United Kingdom's asylum process: as already emphasised above, low recognition rates are not in themselves evidence of such misuse of the asylum process.

Moreover, while the Government has placed much emphasis on this alleged misuse of the asylum process in seeking to justify the new measures, it has so far failed to recognise or acknowledge that this phenomenon - such as it exists - stems directly from the manifest failure of the Asylum & Immigration Act 1993 and the resultant delays and backlogs in the process, for which the Government itself must accept responsibility.

For it is the current excessive delays in the process, caused by gross inefficiency and poor productivity on the part of the Home Office's Asylum Division and an under-resourcing of the asylum appeals system, compounded by the Home Office's general failure to carry out the expulsion of unsuccessful asylum applicants, that creates an incentive for "abusive" asylum applications by those simply seeking to circumvent the United Kingdom's immigration controls or avoid deportation.

As already noted above, it currently takes some 19 months (on average) to fully resolve an asylum application (ie including any appeal). Furthermore, the chances of an unsuccessful applicant being removed (ie expelled) from the United Kingdom at the end of the process are relatively low. In the four year period 1992-95, a total of 66,955 asylum-seekers were refused by the Home Office and approximately 80 per cent of all appeals to the IAA were dismissed. In other words, in this four year period some 54,000 rejected asylum applicants reached the very end of the asylum process and became liable to removal. And yet, during the same period, only 7,902 rejected asylum-seekers were actually removed or made a voluntary departure from the United Kingdom.[19] Clearly, if the chances of being expelled from the United Kingdom after making an unsuccessful asylum application are as little as one in seven, then there is a strong incentive for those seeking only to circumvent the United Kingdom's immigration controls to make an "abusive" asylum claim.

In making this point, Amnesty International is *not* advocating an increase in the

---

19 Sources: Home Office Statistical Bulletin, 15/95; and *Hansard* (House of Commons), 8 February 1996, col. 310 (written answer).

number of removals under the current asylum-determination procedures, which the organisation considers seriously flawed. Given that many of those refused asylum under the existing arrangements have, in Amnesty International's view, been wrongly and unjustly refused, this would only result in direct or indirect breaches of the 1951 UN Convention and other international instruments.

In Amnesty International's view, the proper solution to any problem of "abusive" asylum applications is to substantially reduce the time taken to fully resolve asylum cases (by improving efficiency and therefore productivity, not by removing essential safeguards), and to ensure that those who do not properly qualify for asylum or Exceptional Leave to Remain - *following a full and fair examination of their individual asylum claim* - are actually removed from the United Kingdom at the end of the process. Those aiming to circumvent immigration controls or avoid deportation - the Government's so-called "bogus refugees" - are unlikely to misuse the asylum process in order to enter or remain in the United Kingdom for only one or two months. But it is conceivable that they will do so in order to remain in the United Kingdom for 19 months or more, and in the expectation that - whatever the outcome of their asylum application - they are unlikely to be expelled at the end of the process. As the UN High Commissioner for Refugees (UNHCR) has noted, "under a functional asylum regime, those identified as refugees or given Exceptional Leave to Remain will be promptly given protection and attendant legal and welfare rights. Those who do not qualify can be fairly and expeditiously removed from the country".**20**

---

20 *Certain comments by the UNHCR on the Asylum & Immigration Bill 1995*, issued by the London office of UNHCR in January 1996.

Conclusions

Despite repeated protestations of its commitment to the principles of international refugee law, the United Kingdom Government has embarked on a course of action which Amnesty International believes will seriously undermine its ability to fulfill its obligations under the 1951 UN Convention on Refugees and other international instruments.

It is not disputed that the Government faces serious difficulties in dealing with large numbers of asylum applications, many of which prove not to be well-founded. And the need for a critical examination of all asylum applications is not at issue. But if the Government is fully to meet its obligations under international law, a proper asylum-determination process must exist and, if this process is to work satisfactorily in the long-term, the process must be both fair and efficient. Given the complex and problematic nature of asylum-determination, and the grave consequences of error, it is essential that the process includes effective legal safeguards.

In Amnesty International's view, the implementation of the Asylum & Immigration Bill would result in a substantial diminution of the effectiveness of the legal safeguards established as recently as July 1993. Not only does the Bill provide for a considerable widening of the scope of the existing "fast track" mechanism, which offers insufficient opportunity to challenge an unjust refusal, but - in contravention of international standards - it disables *all* effective legal safeguards in most cases where the applicant arrives not directly from the country of persecution, but via one or more transit countries.

In addition, the Government has enacted new Social Security regulations which deny many needy asylum applicants - including those unjustly refused asylum and seeking to challenge that refusal at appeal - the means to sustain themselves physically while awaiting determination of their asylum claim or appeal. In Amnesty International's view, these Regulations will render meaningless the existence of such legal safeguards as will remain once the Bill has become law.

In seeking to justify these measures, senior Government ministers and others have placed a heavy emphasis on the misuse of the asylum process by those merely seeking to circumvent the United Kingdom's general immigration controls or avoid deportation, and again it is not disputed that this wholly undesirable phenomenon creates very real difficulties for the Government. But those using such arguments have so far failed to recognise that this phenomenon - such as it exists - stems directly from the failings and inefficiencies of the existing arrangements, for which the Government itself must accept responsibility.

Moreover, in focusing solely on the problem of misuse of the asylum process the Government has paid insufficient regard to its obligations, under international law, to those asylum applicants who *are* genuinely fleeing persecution. As the United Nations High Commissioner for Refugees (UNCHR) has noted, the new measures "make it as difficult for genuine refugees to enter the process as those who are not". And the Government cannot claim to be complying with its international obligations while taking steps which have the effect, if not the aim, of restricting the opportunities for those genuinely fleeing persecution to seek and obtain protection in the United Kingdom.

Amnesty International believes that the correct and necessary approach is to address the inefficiencies of the Home Office Asylum Division, and ensure proper resourcing of the process at both the initial stage and the appeal stage. This would involve taking the necessary steps to ensure a substantial improvement in productivity within the Asylum Division - by eradicating inefficient working practices and making better use of computer technology - but additional staff resources may also be required, both within the Asylum Division and within the Immigration Appellate Authority. It would also involve abolishing the as yet undeclared "quota" in the granting of asylum and Exceptional Leave to Remain, and ensuring that all decisions are based on: (a) an objective and detailed assessment of the individual circumstances of the case; and (b) comprehensive information - drawn from the widest possible range of impartial and authoritative information - about the political and human rights situation in the applicant's country of origin. And it would involve the establishment of a credible mechanism for ensuring high standards of legal representation in asylum cases.

Amnesty International recognises that, in an atmosphere of cost-consciousness, there is always likely to be resistance to the idea of committing greater resources to the asylum process. However, the organisation firmly believes that such purely financial considerations should never be used to justify a dilution of the Government's ability to fulfill its obligations under international law. Moreover, the organisation hopes that, on reflection, the Government may yet recognise that taking steps to ensure that the asylum process is both fair and efficient would not only ensure compliance with international law, but would also yield substantial cost savings. Reducing the average time taken to make an initial decision or determine an appeal, for example, would deliver concomitant savings in the Social Security budget. And taking steps to ensure fair and correct decision-making at the initial stage would diminish the necessity of correcting mistakes through the appeals procedure. As the former Home Office minister, Charles Wardle MP, has put it: "if one wants to remove large chunks of overhead, one sometimes has to spend first in order to realise savings".[1] And, of course, ensuring that all asylum claims are resolved as expeditiously as is consistent with the need to identify, and protect, all those applicants who merit the granting of asylum would also remove the very incentive for misuse of the process, leading to yet further cost savings.

---

1 *Hansard* (House of Commons), 11 December 1995, col. 748.

PLAYING HUMAN PINBALL
Home Office Practice in "Safe Third Country" Asylum Cases

In July 1993 the Government enacted new legislation - the Asylum & Immigration Appeals Act - providing for stricter application of the criteria for granting asylum and the rapid expulsion of rejected asylum-seekers. Despite no apparent change in the nature of applications, the proportion of successful applicants has since fallen substantially.

In particular, the 1993 Act established a special "fast-track" procedure enabling the Home Office to seek to "pass the buck" by returning asylum-seekers to so-called safe third countries - that is, countries through which they passed in transit to the United Kingdom and where, it is held, they should have sought asylum - without examining their asylum claims and without any guarantee that the "third country" in question will do so.

This report - based on a nine-month study of 60 individual cases - demonstrates that this "fast-track" procedure has failed to perform to the Government's expectations: intended to allow for the expulsion of asylum-seekers to "third countries" within "a week to 10 days", the procedure has proven to be neither rapid nor productive in terms of expulsions. It shows that the procedure imposes immense hardship on those unfortunate enough to fall within its scope. It indicates that this game of "human pinball" compromises the Government's upholding of its obligations under the 1951 UN Convention on Refugees. And it concludes that, unless the Government is willing to introduce proper safeguards, such practice - and the "fast-track" procedure itself - should be abandoned and the millions of pounds it costs every year put to better use

Price £7.99.

1873328176 Published June 1995 pp85

PRISONERS WITHOUT A VOICE
Asylum-Seekers Detained in the United Kingdom
Second revised and expanded edition

In October 1994 Amnesty International UK published the first edition of this report. It demonstrated that a lack of accountability and absence of judicial control over the decision to detain asylum-seekers results in arbitrary decision making and, in at least 44% of cases, unnecessary detention.

In the wake of its publication junior Home Office Minister, Nicholas Baker, was forced to reveal for the first time that the average cost of holding an asylum seeker in an immigration detention centre is "over £800 per week" and in a criminal prison £422 per week. Using these figures Amnesty International has calculated that the cost of detaining asylum-seekers is about £20million per annum.

This important report has been fully revised, expanded and updated to include the government's response to Amnesty International's recommendations.

Price £7.99

1873328117 Originally Published October 1994, New edition published May 1995 pp82

For more information about Amnesty International publishing, send an A5 stamped addressed envelope to: Amnesty International Publishing, 99-119, Rosebery Avenue, London EC1R 4RE. Tel: 0171 814 6200, Fax: 0171 833 1510, email: bookshop@ai-uk.gn.apc.org

The latest information on Amnesty Publishing is available on the internet. Point your browser at http://www.oneworld.org/amnesty/.

THE WORK OF AMNESTY INTERNATIONAL

Amnesty International is a worldwide voluntary movement that works to prevent some of the gravest violations by governments of people's fundamental human rights. The main focus of its campaigning is to :

- *free all prisoners of conscience* - those detained anywhere solely for their beliefs, or because of their ethnic origin, sex, colour or language - who have not used or advocated violence;

- *ensure fair and prompt trials for political prisoners;*

- abolish the death penalty, torture and other cruel treatment of prisoners;

- end extra-judicial executions and "disappearances".

Amnesty International also opposes abuses by opposition groups: hostage taking; torture and killings of prisoners and other arbitrary killings.

Amnesty International, recognising that human rights are indivisible and interdependent, works to promote all the human rights enshrined in the Universal Declaration of Human Rights and other international standards through its human rights education programme and through campaigning for ratification of human rights treaties.

Amnesty International is impartial. It is independent of any government, political persuasion or religious creed. It does not support or oppose any government or political system nor does it support or oppose the views of the victims whose rights it seeks to protect. It is concerned solely with the protection of the human rights involved in each case, regardless of the ideology of the government, opposition forces or the beliefs of the individual.

Amnesty International does not grade countries according to their record on human rights; instead of attempting comparisons it concentrates on trying to end the specific violations of human rights in each case.

Amnesty International has formal relations with the United Nations Economic and Social Council (ECOSOC); the United Nations Educational, Scientific and Cultural Organisation (UNESCO); the Council of Europe; the Organisation of American States; the Organisation of African Unity and the Inter-Parliamentary Union.

Amnesty International is financed by subscriptions and donations from its world-wide membership. No funds are sought or accepted from governments. To safeguard the independence of the organisation, all contributions are strictly controlled by guidelines laid down by the International Council.

Amnesty International at the start of 1995 had more than 1,100,000 members and subscribers in 150 countries. It had 8,000 local groups in more than 70 countries in Africa, the Americas, Asia, Europe and the Middle East. In the United Kingdom the organisation had 116,000 members, 330 local groups and 15 specialised networks.